Contents

Acknowledgements

This volume has emerged out of discussions and seminars held at the European Centre for the Study of Policing at the Open University. We would like to thank all those colleagues – fellow academics, police officers and others – who have participated. We would particularly like to thank Philippe Robert and the Groupe Européen de Recherche sur les Normativités for encouraging our interest and contributing to the expenses of an Interlabo conference in October 1997. Finally our thanks to Sabine Phillips for her administrative and translating assistance within the Centre.

Richard Bessel
Clive Emsley
Milton Keynes and York
September 1998

Introduction

Clive Emsley and Richard Bessel

On Saturday 11 October 1997 the England football team played a World Cup qualifying match against Italy in the Olympic Stadium in Rome. Within minutes of the kick-off an even rougher confrontation started off the pitch. For Antonio de Greco, the commander of *La Celere*, the specially trained riot squads of the Italian police involved in the fighting, the conflict off the pitch provided a new experience: 'Normally in Italy after a baton charge or two the problems end, but with the English we had to keep going and going.'[1] The narratives of English supporters quoted in the national press told a different story. 'It was extremely brutal', a marketing manager among them told a reporter for *The Times*. 'The police were clearly terrified and had been wound up to the point where they were treating us as if we were all hooligans. There were 20 to 30 English fans causing trouble and they should have been sorted out.' A woman barrister with the supporters protested that 'the police behaviour was indefensible.'[2] Yet another supporter, who had gone to the match with his wife, a merchant-banker friend and his son, wrote a newspaper article describing his experiences. 'It was the kind of approach to crowd control that I had witnessed on the streets of Jakarta. Not what I would have expected of a democratic European partner.'[3] The head of the Labour Government's Football Task Force, himself a former Conservative minister, agreed: 'That was not the behaviour of a civilised police force.'[4]

Barristers, marketing managers and merchant bankers are not the kind of individuals generally associated with English soccer supporters; but nor are they the kind of people who, in liberal western democracies, are often at the receiving end of a police-

1

man's baton. When such individuals are involved, and, as in this case, when instances of disorder are given a high profile by the media, then there can be heated debate about police attitudes and behaviour, about their preparedness and training. The novel element in Rome in October 1997 was the fact that the supporters were English and the police were Italian. The latter were probably keyed up by the fear of the unenviable reputation of English football fans – in the words of *Corriere della Sera* the fans were 'built like wardrobes, with arms carpeted with tattoos, bloated stomachs and killer breath. … They adore beer, love violence'.[5] And, while there seems little doubt that the Italian police did overreact, part of the outrage expressed in England was laced with a perception of the noble traditions of the British bobby. 'Italy has much to learn about British police techniques of isolating troublemakers and taking them out of the stands at the first sign of trouble' declared *The Times*.[6] *The Independent* was rather more restrained: 'the [British] police have got their act together'. But then went on to warn about xenophobic prejudices: 'not all Italian policeman are wonderful, but neither are all of them practising for a role in the Taviani Brothers forthcoming epic of *Il Duce and his Blackshirts*'.[7]

Over the last thirty years social scientists and social historians have stressed the need to take popular protest and rioting seriously. The corollary of this, which seems less well acknowledged, is the need to take the policing of protest and rioting seriously.[8] 'Legitimising notions' may play a significant role in large-scale public disorder, in the sense that individuals do not usually demonstrate without some significant cause uniting them and prompting them.[9] Equally, large-scale disorder may, in part, be the result of frustrations and feelings of disenfranchisement. John Bohstedt, a historian of English riots during the late eighteenth and early nineteenth centuries, has described the phenomenon as 'community politics' with the unenfranchised calling the attention of those with power within the state – both local and central – to immediate and pressing problems. He used a similar analysis to explain (though not excuse) the ferocious conflict which erupted on the Broadwater Farm Estate in North London in October 1985, during which P.C. Keith Blakelock was hacked to death by the rioters and English police for the first time deployed, though did not use, plastic bullets. 'Riots are the politics of the excluded,' wrote Bohstedt. 'Until the communities from which riots spring have gained political recognition and representation, riots will continue. … The police have been the triggers and targets of riots because they are the face of an alien power structure.'[10] All of this puts the police into an essentially passive role; some of their activities, indeed their very presence, may 'trigger' riot, and then they naturally become 'targets' as the representatives of authority. But which policing activities provoke trouble, and in what contexts? This raises a further question: have the experiences been similar across different national contexts with different kinds of police and political regime? Can we indeed speak of 'patterns of provocation' that police fall into at various times and in various places?

The aim of this volume is to examine in depth a cross section of incidents of public disorder taken from different national contexts in the interwar and postwar years. The authors are historians and social scientists approaching the issues from their respective academic standpoints, but drawing on each other's expertise. The principal focus is less on the disorder itself than on the role and behaviour of the police involved, and precisely how they might have become the triggers for trouble. The evidence that follows suggests that some common patterns are detectable in very diverse political regimes. On the one hand, a mishandled arrest, the rapid spread of rumours about police brutality, the escalation of hostility, can culminate in a major instance of public disorder; this can be seen both in the Saalfeld disorder in the dictatorial socialist German Democratic Republic in 1951 (chapter 4) and in the Harlem riot in the liberal capitalist United States in 1964 (chapter 5). On the other, heightened tension among the police, and the expectation of serious disorder, can be ignited by a spark into an explosion of police violence; Berlin's 'Blutmai' of 1929 (chapter 1) and the *Affaire de Clichy* in Paris in 1937 (chapter 2) provide examples here, and it is at least arguable that some of the more extreme confrontations during the British miners' strike of 1984–85 had similar causes (chapter 6).

Common explanations and solutions have been offered by the authorities, often regardless of the actual occasion of the violence. Riots have invariably been attributed to 'agitators'; less commonly, they are acknowledged to have been provoked by the clumsy behaviour of a policeman, but a policeman who is a 'rotten apple' or a 'black sheep'. Of course agitators exist, and the Clichy affair appears to have had more than the usual share, but the allegation of the ubiquitous agitator prompting and provoking every incident of serious disorder is undermined by the infrequency of the appearance of such individuals in court. The concepts of the 'legitimising notion' and 'community politics' are better born out by the evidence. The 'rotten apple' policeman may provide a legitimising notion for a crowd, but again such individuals have rarely been identified, let alone disciplined. Moreover it could be argued that the root of many instances of disorder is to be found more in the cultures and structures of the police institutions than simply in the fault of single, undesirable individuals within the ranks.

Max Weber famously defined a state as that collectivity of institutions enjoying a monopoly of legitimate violence within a continuously bounded territory. The police officer is the only individual legally authorised to use such force in his day-to-day dealings with the population of the state. David H. Bayley, describing how the modern police divide into specialised sections, warned that these specialisms should not be confused with definitions of 'police'. He emphasised that other state agencies are empowered to enforce laws and this led him to conclude that the basic definition of 'a specialised police force' is its concentration 'on the application of force': Policing becomes specialised when agencies are directed to concentrate primarily on the application of physical force.'[11] The French sociologist, François Dieu, in turn, has sketched a typology of the violent force employed by policemen: *la violence instrumentale*, used by the police for tasks justified by their legitimate authority; *la violence dérivée*, a by-product of the former when individual policemen are carried away by panic or accident and strike out unjustifiably at those who just happen to get in the way; and *la violence déviante*, which is, by definition, inexcusable offending.[12] It would be convenient and comforting to think that it is only the latter two, and especially *la violence déviante*, which trigger disorder and/or hostility to the police and challenge their legitimacy, but this probably is not the case.

If policemen are encouraged as a group to view agitators and disturbers of the peace as political subversives, as members of a dangerous class or as inferiors, possibly because of their ethnic origins, then it scarcely needs a 'rotten apple' to trigger disorder. Such encouragement might emerge, for example, from an influential politician indicating an 'enemy within' as well as from racist, peer group banter. On 17 October 1961, as the ferocious Algerian War of Independence drew to its close, a demonstration was organised in Paris by Algerians to protest against a recent curfew imposed upon them. Officially three protesters died at the hands of the Parisian police. However, the true figure appears to have been at least fifty, and there remains dispute over the extent to which Maurice Papon, the Prefect of Police, and other senior officers gave tacit approval to the men's actions. Political pressure was exerted to keep the extent of the events of October 1961 under wraps,[13] and, whatever the extant of Papon's involvement or that of his senior officers, this probably has to be categorised as *la violence déviante*.

Nevertheless, it remains possible for heavy-handed but legally legitimate police action to provoke serious community resistance. A police raid on a black-owned café in the St. Pauls district of Bristol in April 1980 provoked serious rioting and compelled the police to withdraw temporarily from the area. The raid was lawful in itself but, in his report to the Home Secretary, the chief constable of Avon and Somerset, within whose jurisdiction the city of Bristol fell, admitted a series of errors in the timing, the use of drug dogs, and the failure to consult the local police community relations officer, all of which appear to have contributed to the hostility towards, and the eventual attacks on the police.[14] Critics of the so-called 'Zero Tolerance' principle, credited with reducing crime in New York City, revealed an awareness which might well have been learned from the St Pauls affair. 'What [people] do not want to see', wrote the chief constable of the Thames Valley Police, 'is police officers who feel no allegiance to their community, who appear to have no discretion about arresting or prosecuting offenders, and whose "Zero Tolerance" attitude is dictatorial, inflexible and oppressive. It is these very features which, when they have occurred in British policing history (for example, in the 1980s), have alienated the community and resulted in corruption and riots.'[15]

When policemen confront mass disorder, but are not properly trained for dealing with it, a shambles can result. In 1964 the New York Police Department had an elite unit of young, big men and recently updated riot control plans; but this tactical unit was too small, the plans appear to have existed only on paper, and patrolmen found themselves isolated in small groups. Possibly because of the outrage provoked by the use of tear-gas, water cannon and dogs during a civil rights march in Alabama the year earlier, the patrolmen responded to the riot by firing their guns over the heads of the rioters; in spite of the enormous expenditure of bullets, probably more by luck than judgement there were remarkably few casualties. Yet, having men prepared and trained for dealing with riots does not necessarily ensure that situations are well handled. The police in 1920s Berlin had been trained to deal with a rising of Communist workers, and certain working-class districts had been targeted as the likely centres of trouble. When disorder erupted in May 1929 it was not such a rising, but the police response was more in accordance with what they had expected than with what they actually faced; the result was significant loss of life. The police deployed in Clichy in 1937 were prepared and care had been taken to separate the riot squads from demonstrators with a line of ordinary police. Quite how the disorder initially erupted here remains a matter of dispute; and Clichy illustrates a further problem: it was possible to plan for a demonstration in advance, but it was impossible to dispatch reinforcements with a clear briefing of what to do and how to do it. There too frightened policemen reached for their guns.

In few states has the use of firearms been considered as anything other than a means of last resort for dealing with riot and disorder. In eighteenth-century England, where the military was the only permanently organised agency available for the suppression of riot, considerable efforts were made to avoid the use of deadly force.[16] Since the eighteenth century the weaponry available to the state has become considerably more lethal and more effective, yet there has been a reluctance to sanction its use against rioters. The German Democratic Republic may have been a repressive Marxist-Leninist tyranny, but the police did not use their guns on the Saalfeld miners in 1951; the GDR professed itself a workers' state, and there was a great reluctance for police to fire on those heroic exemplars of the working class, the miners. In both the 'people's democracies' and liberal democracies alternative means were developed for the suppression of disorder in the shape of water cannon, plastic bullets, shields, longer batons and armour for the police. Chief officers also argued the need for professional training, as well as for proper equipment and for planning. However, while it may be possible to plan for disorder emerging from an organised demonstration, it is much more difficult to plan for any trouble erupting from a specific, but unexpected incident.

Moreover, equipping and training for riots in itself may aggravate trouble. The 'Blutmai' incident described by Peter Leßmann-Faust provides an example of where training, and the linked expectations, contributed to police overreaction. Of course, it might be argued that the Berlin Police in 1929 were acting in a context of political tension; it had been only a little over ten years since Berlin had witnessed revolution, and street gangs of left and right were frequently in conflict with each other. In Britain throughout the 1970s and early 1980s there was talk of a political crisis; terrorism in Northern Ireland spilled over into England, strikers and the underprivileged in inner cities clashed with the police, and the police developed new, paramilitary tactics. The tactics and equipment were justified on the grounds of unprecedented disorder and threats to state and society; supporters of the new techniques insisted that professional, well-trained, highly disciplined public order specialists, in control of themselves and under the control of their superiors, constituted the best solution to the problems. Critics argued that there was a gap between the professionalism which was invoked and the reality of paramilitary policing that tended to amplify the prospect of disorder. Furthermore it appeared that, far from their being professional and controlled, when police trained in paramilitary methods and issued with special riot equipment were let loose, 'control' and 'professionalism' appeared to be among the first casualties.[17] Of course, this is a general problem, which faces trained soldiers no less than trained policemen: how does one reflect 'professional' training when directly applying physical force?

Wherever police function their behaviour is, in theory, controlled by norms, by laws and regulations. Rioting and popular disorder have commonly resulted in court cases, and courts have often been reluctant to sanction or to seek to regulate future police behaviour in the light of evidence presented. In the context of fear of revolution, as in Berlin in 1929, or of a colonial war which threatened the internal security of the imperial power, as in Paris in 1961, this might have been understandable, though hardly excusable. Yet even the proudest liberal democracies, even in peacetime, have not been averse to giving preference to police evidence and justifications. For example, from the events in Glasgow in the 1930s described by Andrew Davies (chapter 3), it would appear that the gang-busting chief constable Percy Sillitoe engineered an incident so as to teach the city's gangs a lesson and that the courts went along with the partial police account, which obscured such an intention.

Of course, if the courts cease to support the police, then police morale can crumble and the institution may become lax in responding to threats to the existing political and social order. Such appears to have been the case with the Prussian police in the peculiar political situation towards the end of the Weimar Republic.[18] However, blanket support for police action by the courts and failure to investigate or even acknowledge potential police wrongdoing can foster public cynicism as well as the kind of alienation among oppressed and/or disenfranchised groups which, in turn, contributes to popular disorder. Policing is not, and never has been an easy task, especially when it concerns high profile incidents of public disorder. The essays which follow deal commonly with police errors, not because of any partisan attitudes about police in general, but rather to emphasise first, that there are difficulties and sensitivies surrounding police tasks that have similarities across widely differing regimes; second, that the police have to be recognised as actors in the potential for disorder and not as an instrument simply responding to disorder; and third, that the legitimacy of regimes and of police institutions remains a matter of negotiation.

Finally, as Dominique Wisler and Marco Tackenberg urge (chapter 7), the question of the role of the police in controlling or provoking disorder, cannot be reduced simply to studying the interactions between police and demonstrators. Such disorders are also fought out in the public sphere, through the media and political debate; subsequently they can also, as in this volume, be refought by academic observers. The outcome of this revisiting of disorder can be crucial for the police. The immediate discussion, with its reconstruction of events and apportioning of blame, can set new constraints on the behaviour of demonstrators, police, or both, which is significant for any renewal of confrontation. The more considered discussion, whether or not a consensus is reached, should, if nothing else, warn against any complacency even in those societies boasting 'the best police in the world'.

Notes

1. Quoted in *The Daily Telegraph*, 13 October 1997, p. 1, and for a slightly different translation see *The Guardian*, 13 October 1997, p. 3.
2. *The Times*, 13 October 1997, p. 3.
3. William Sieghart, 'Battering of the Innocents', *The Times*, 14 October 1997, p. 20.
4. David Mellor, quoted on p. 1 of *The Daily Telegraph*, 13 October 1997.
5. Quoted in *The Guardian*, 13 October 1997, p. 3.
6. Leading article, *The Times*, 14 October 1997, p. 21.
7. Leading article, *The Independent*, 14 October 1997, p. 20.
8. The exception here is P.A.J. Waddington, *Liberty and Order: Public Order Policing in a Capital City* (London, 1994).
9. For the concept of 'legitimising notions' see E.P. Thompson, 'The Moral Economy of the English Crowd in the Eighteenth Century', in E.P. Thompson, *Customs in Common* (London, 1991).
10. John Bohstedt, *Riots and Community Politics in England and Wales, 1790–1810* (Cambridge Mass., 1983). Letter from Bohstedt to *The Times*, 4 November 1985, p. 13.
11. David H. Bayley, *Patterns of Policing: A Comparative International Analysis* (New Brunswick, N.J., 1985), pp. 12–13.
12. François Dieu, 'Eléments pour une approche socio-politique dans la violence policière', *Déviance et société*, vol. xix (1995), 35–49.
13. Georges Carrot, himself a former senior officer of the Police Nationale, devoted seven lines to the incident in his massive *Le maintien de l'ordre en France:*

Depuis la fin de l'ancien régime jusqu'au 1968, 2 vols. (Toulouse, 1984), vol. 2. p. 813. He gives a bald statement to the effect that there was some disorder, and gives an official death toll of two.

14. Tony Jefferson and Roger Grimshaw, *Controlling the Constable: Police Accountability in England and Wales* (London, 1984), pp. 78–9.

15. Charles Pollard, 'Zero Tolerance; Short-term Fix, Long-tern Liability?' in Norman Dennis (ed.), *Zero Tolerance: Policing a Free Society*, (London, 1997), pp. 57–8.

16. Tony Hayter, *The Army and the Crowd in Mid-Georgian England* (London, 1978), pp. 176–85.

17. The most cogent cases, on each side of the argument, are to be found respectively in Tony Jefferson, *The Case against Paramilitary Policing* (Milton Keynes, 1990), and P.A.J. Waddington, *The Strong Arm of the Law: Armed Police and Public Order Policing* (Oxford, 1991).

18. Peter Leßmann-Faust, '"Au poste perdu". La police en Prusse 1930–1933', in Jean Marc Berlière and Denis Peschanski (eds.), *Pouvoirs et polices au XXe siècle: Europe, Etats-Unis et Japon* (Brussels, 1997).

1

'Blood May':
The Case of Berlin 1929

Peter Leßmann-Faust

In his recent the history of Communists in the Weimar Republic,[1] Klaus-Michael Mallmann writes of the 'police shooting orgy of the "Blutmai" [Blood May] in 1929' that in its 'deeply symbolic power and poisonous effect [it] can best be compared with the murder of [Rosa] Luxemburg and [Karl] Liebknecht' in 1919.[2] Although this puts the four days of street-fighting in Berlin in May 1929 on par with one of the fundamental disasters of the Weimar Republic and the Communist movement at the time, at no point in his book does Mallmann examine the Berlin 'Blutmai' of 1929 closely. This discrepancy seems to me symptomatic of both the conspicuous historical importance of the events in Berlin during May 1929 and the hesitancy of historians in dealing with this incident.

In the 'classic' historiography of the Communist Party of Germany (KPD) in the Weimar Republic the street battles of 1–4 May 1929 between police, demonstrators and innocent members of the public – fighting which had been provoked by Berlin Police President Karl Zörgiebel's ban on marches and demonstrations on May Day and which left behind many dead and injured – served as a 'catalyst for ultra-left politics' by the KPD,[3] clearing the path for the acceptance of the 'social fascism' thesis by the Party membership.[4] Leading functionaries of the KPD believed the Party after 1 May 1929 to be in a phase 'of a new revolutionary upturn', of the 'radicalisation and revolutionising of the masses' and the 'accelerated process of abandonment by the masses of traitorous Social Democracy'.[5]

Its revolutionary slogans notwithstanding, the KPD had not made preparations for a revolutionary situation, to say nothing of offering propaganda which corresponded to social reality.[6] The noisy agitation of the KPD leading up to the events of May, the call for public transport strikes, and talk even of the 'overthrowing of the government' found no corresponding preparations for an escalation or even the beginning of the desired revolutionary situation. The bloody events beginning at midday on 1 May found the KPD and its street-agitation troops, the *Roter Frontkämpferbund* (RFB, Red Front-fighters League) completely unprepared;[7] calls for mass demonstrations and strikes met with no success.[8] Indeed there are indications that the KPD had scarcely any influence over the street fighters and barricade builders at the main trouble spots in the Berlin May battles, rather that the motivation of the numerous young street fighters to defend proletarian 'territory' and to enjoy challenging the overtaxed police played a large role.[9]

The May events in Berlin were no page of glory for the Prussian Government, and specifically for the Social Democratic Prussian Minister of the Interior Albert Grzesinski and the Social Democratic Police President of Berlin Karl Zörgiebel. These two men bore a large portion of the responsibility for the confrontations as a result of their ban on demonstrations on May Day 1929 – the only such ban proclaimed on this traditional holiday of the workers movement in the entire German Reich in 1929! In addition their remarks about the behaviour of the police, their attempts, couched in martial language, to assume 'political responsibility' for the incidents and to 'cover' for the police, cast harsh light on policing policy in democratic Prussia, which up to 1929 had been praised by many political observers.[10] Serious discussions and analyses of Social Democratic policing policy in Prussia following the event, particularly by the government itself, did not materialise: 'In the Prussian Cabinet the events were not discussed'.[11] Restrained criticism voiced by Grzesinski's and Zörgiebel's party colleagues was short-lived;[12] and for the Social Democratic Party (SPD), the Blood May was altogether only an episode without great significance.[13]

Indeed in spite of his share of responsibility for the Blood May, Albert Grzesinski's reputation has not suffered in the historiography of the period.[14] Until recently the same held for the Prussian policing policy in the Weimar Republic in general.[15] Blood May exists so to speak as an anomaly in the history of the Weimar

Republic; it is an irritating solitary incident among the many successive events which accompanied the state crisis of the Weimar Republic, an incident the ordering and explanation of which historians find problematical.[16]

In my opinion dealing with the events in Berlin in May 1929 mainly from the perspective of party-political or cabinet history will not lead to an explanation of the historical problem of Blood May. One has to focus on the incident and be able to explain it as it already had appeared to some contemporary observers: as a 'police catastrophe',[17] as an illuminating and, to the public at the time, astonishing revelation of the results of the reorganisation and reorientation of the Prussian uniformed police after 1919.

The Prehistory of Blood May

After 1919 the Governments of the Reich and Prussia lived in fear of a large-scale attempt by the KPD to rekindle the revolution which had been cut short in 1918–19; the KPD never tired of conjuring up the revolution's final victory in its propaganda. The revolutionary avant-garde of the KPD, its cadre for building a 'Red Army' in Germany, was believed to be the *Roter Frontkämpferbund*. The attempts by Prussian Interior Minister Grzesinski to dissolve the RFB reached their climax during the Blood May.

The KPD had founded the *Roter Frontkämpferbund* in the summer of 1924, following the aborted attempts at revolution in 1923.[18] The RFB was not intended to serve the KPD leadership as a revolutionary army in a violent overthrow of the government, but to prepare for political mass confrontations within the framework of the Weimar constitution.[19] As a Communist war-veterans organisation, the RFB was intended to preserve the military attitudes of the many Communist ex-servicemen of the World War, but for agitation on the streets, not for military action in the service of the KPD.[20] As an appendage of the politically isolated KPD, the RFB with its 106,000 members in 1928[21] was subject to close scrutiny by the Reich and Land governments. It enjoyed no political protection in high places, as did the Social Democratic *Reichsbanner* and, particularly, the conservative *Stahlhelm*. (The street-fighting army of the Nazi Party (NSDAP), the 'SA' (*Sturm-Abteilungen*, Storm Sections) was taken particularly seriously neither by government nor by the KPD before the end of the 1920s; until the Reichtag elections of 14 September 1930 the NSDAP was dismissed as an also ran.[22])

From August 1925 the Reich Government pressed the Länder to agree jointly on a nationwide ban of the RFB. Prussia withheld its approval, because the Reich Interior Minister did not agree to the dissolution of some local *Stahlhelm* groups which had attracted attention by their illegal use of weapons. Albert Grzesinski, who had succeeded Carl Severing as Prussian Interior Minister on 6 October 1926, rejected the request of Reich Interior Minister Walther von Kedell (German National People's Party) to the Land governments for a ban on 17 April 1928 for electoral reasons. Grzesinski feared that banning the RFB before the Reichstag elections of 20 May 1928 would give the KPD a propaganda advantage and an excuse to contest the election result. Nevertheless, prohibiting the RFB, SA and the *Stahlhelm* was often the subject of discussions in the spring of 1928 between Grzesinski and Prussia's Social Democratic Prime Minister Otto Braun.[23]

The abrupt turn of the KPD against the SPD within the framework of the 'ultra left strategy' that the party propagated in early 1928, and that led to the notorious 'social fascism' thesis,[24] caused the Prussian Government to shy away from treating the RFB in a pragmatic and detached manner. Because there had been serious clashes between the police and a marching section of the RFB after the Reich elections of May 1928 and a day before the fourth national rally of the RFB in Berlin, Grzesinski ordered a memorandum be drawn up to prepare for a ban of the RFB. Interestingly enough it was a concession to Adolf Hitler that contributed to the escalation of the Blood May of 1929. On 28 September 1928 Grzesinski lifted the ban, in place since September 1925, on Adolf Hitler speaking publicly in Prussia. According to the previous Prussian Interior Minister Carl Severing, who disapproved of his successor's decision, Grzesinski justified lifting the ban by pointing out that the Nazi Party was no longer of political significance.[25] After Hitler's first speech following the lifting of the ban, on 16 November 1928 in the Berlin Sports Palace, there were a number of clashes between Communists and Nazis, resulting in three deaths.[26] This provided the justification for a police ban on demonstrations in Berlin from 13 December 1928, and it was this ban which the KPD broke on 1 May 1929, provoking the Blood May. The December ban on demonstrations led Berlin Police President Zörgiebel to prohibit the traditional memorial rallies at the graves of Karl Liebknecht and Rosa Luxemburg in January 1929. On 21 March 1929 Grzesinski warned 'once again very seriously' all the political formations to contribute to the pacification of political life, allowed the local and regional authorities to ban outdoor meetings, and let it be known that organisations which continued to behave radically would be dissolved.[27] This warning was regarded by the KPD, with good reason,[28] as a threat to ban the RFB.

Given these circumstances, in the run-up to the demonstrations and rallies which both the SPD and KPD regularly held on the May Day and to the RFB's national rally planned for 20 May, an explosive mood developed within the KPD. On 25 March the leaders of the RFB called for a 'mass mobilisation against the disgraceful plans of the social-fascist lackeys' of the 'bourgeoisie'. In April the KPD prophesied that the 'revolutionary élan of the German workers' would demonstrate to the 'Police Minister of the Trust Bourgeoisie' that the proletariat did not 'give a damn' for his bans.[29] Fourteen days before the May Day, which was then not yet a statutory holiday, police formations were put on alert in all Berlin's police stations.[30] The 14,000 regular police in Berlin, a city of four million inhabitants, stood ready for action.

The Blood May in Berlin, 1 to 4 May 1929

On the evening of 30 April youths assaulted traffic police at several locations in the city.[31] By the early morning hours of 1 May clashes already had occurred in most of Berlin's districts, the largest number in Wedding, Neukölln and the Hackescher Markt in the District Mitte, between groups of demonstrators assembling for rallies and marches and the police.[32] Demonstrators hurled insults at police officers and tried to disrupt street traffic by cutting the overhead wires of trams or throwing building material, which had been assembled for the extension of the underground line in Neukölln's Hermannstraße, into the streets. The police retaliated with truncheons and, increasingly, with 'warning shots' against demonstrators, onlookers and innocent passers-by.

Around midday the first two fatalities occurred. On the Hackescher Markt six policemen felt themselves threatened by several demonstrators who approached them from nearby streets. One of the police, pistol drawn, attempted to arrest one of the apparent ringleaders, but was pulled down by him and insulted while the surrounding demonstrators applauded. The police then indiscriminately fired several shots into the crowd. One demonstrator was killed after being hit three times; four others were slightly wounded. In Wedding, while clearing the Kösliner Straße, police were bombarded with missiles thrown from windows of the surrounding houses and called 'bloodhounds'. The police ordered that all windows be shut, otherwise shots would be fired. A thirty-two-year-old artisan disobeyed, because he wanted to speak to the police. One of the policemen aimed at the man's forehead and killed him.

Soon after news of the Wedding incident spread, the first barricades were erected in the neighbouring streets and policemen were attacked with missiles from the rooftops. In the afternoon and evening, as the KPD, SPD and trade union rallies came to an end and returning day-trippers crowded onto the streets, the confrontations escalated. A limping war invalid seeking cover behind a door in the Kösliner Straße was wounded by a policeman who, 'aiming from a crouched position', shot him through the door panel. The man bled to death because the police ignored him and ambulance personnel were unable to reach him until an hour later.[33]

Another serious confrontation occurred that evening in the police station on the Landsberger Platz in the district of Friedrichshain. The men in the station had been on alert for the previous fortnight and on 1 May were strengthened by two squads from the Friedrichshain district police headquarters; there were now about 200 officers there. During the day the men had broken up twenty-five banned rallies while suffering verbal abuse and physical attack from the demonstrators. They had frustrated attempts by demonstrators to form marching columns, and repeatedly prevented the building of barricades near the police station. Around the time when the first news of alleged exchanges of fire in Wedding and Neukölln reached the station, seven members of the Friedrichshain *Arbeiterschützenbund* (Workers' Rifle Association) were walking across the Landsberger Platz. They had attended a shooting competition as part of the May Day festivities and were carrying their air rifles over their shoulders, wrapped in cloth cases. These seven men, without resisting, were arrested by the police and taken to the station. Before they arrived, however, the rumour had spread amongst the police that 'Communists were about to storm the station and that seven men with rifles and one machine gun already had been arrested'.[34] The arrested workers were greeted at the station with the call: 'Here are the dogs from Wedding!'. Although it was easy enough to establish that they had carried only air rifles, the workers had to run the gauntlet and were beaten unconscious.[35]

The battles continued over the following three days. Police were verbally abused and had objects thrown at them; during the nights barricades were erected in the working-class districts of Wedding and Neukölln, near the Hermannstraße. Police patrols broke up 'suspicious' gatherings, searched house entrances or fired machine guns and carbines from armoured cars over the heads of passers-by. The police pursued and arrested passers-by, people waiting at tram stops on their way to work, standing at traffic intersections and in shops. The telephone diary of the police command includes the entry on 1 May: '20:40. Mr X, Reinickendorfer Straße, rings and complains about the methods of the local police. He has urgent business to attend to and cannot leave his flat. A window in his flat has been broken by gunshot'. On 2 May the Criminal Investigation Police at the Berlin Police Presidium recorded the following message: 'At around 14.30 the lorry driver X rang the telephone exchange excitedly and requested in the name of the tenants of the building at Pankstraße 90 that the house not be fired on any more during the coming evening, as the tenants were terribly upset after yesterday's events'.[36] On the evening of 2 May 'the police had to cut short the deployment of armoured vehicles in Neukölln's Hermannstraße, because a cinema performance had just ended and people were pouring out onto the streets'.[37] On 3 May the police shot and killed three women, including a sixty-year-old on an upper-floor balcony of a building in the Hermannstraße.[38]

On 3 May Police Chief Zörgiebel ordered a 'traffic and lights ban' for some streets in Wedding and Neukölln, a ban which prohibited 'all loitering in hallways, recesses and entrance gates' and which entitled the police to arrest 'people who walked on the streets without a definite aim. … All persons who do not obey these orders put their lives at risk.'[39] In the opinion of the Berlin police leadership the 'traffic and lights ban', together with the state of siege proclaimed at the same time for the districts in question, comprised the last means of getting the unrest under control. Behind the whole affair they suspected a well-prepared strategy of the KPD, although in the night of 2–3 May the KPD leadership had forbidden all further demonstrations and attempts to provoke confrontation – something of which the police, thanks to undercover reports they had received, must have been aware by the morning of 3 May.[40]

The clashes and rioting already were declining on 2 May as compared with the day before. Eighteen civilians met their deaths on 1 May and two on the 2nd (compared with thirteen police injured on 1 May and none injured on the 2nd). However, from midday on 3 May the clashes escalated considerably. By late evening twelve more civilians had been killed, while the police suffered neither dead nor injured. There are some indications that, after the clashes over the previous days, the police now wholly viewed themselves as fighting a war in which they should make 'short work' of their enemies. In the report of a journalist on 3 May one reads:

> It is exactly 12 noon. The silence is ... suddenly broken by the crackling of a machine gun. An armoured vehicle suddenly appears on the street coming from the Hermannplatz, followed by two squad cars. ... Everybody runs and flees into the blocks of flats. ... There was no warning. ... Between Jägerstraße and Ziethenstraße the police detachment halts. The squad jumps from the vehicles, gets their guns ready, and the first shots already are cracking over the heads of the still unsuspecting population. ...'[41]

According to a report from the Police Group South-East (responsible for Neukölln), the police requested and received permission 'to take a squad car and clear the Hermannstraße ruthlessly and once and for all'. Police 'assault troops' were formed. A journalist who asked a policeman the location of his superior received the answer: 'The captain is somewhere in the field.' At the entrance to streets cordoned off by the police placards were placed reminiscent of the revolutionary confrontations of 1918–19, with the slogan: 'Halt, we will shoot'. For the night of 3 to 4 May the police had the 'explicit order to shoot all civilians who were heading for the barricades'. During the night police stationed on roof tops shot into 'rooms and kitchens with lights on in the interior courtyards [of Berlin's working-class housing blocks]'. The last death of the Blood May was that of the New Zealand journalist Charles Mackay, who was shot by a policeman at around 11.00 p.m. on 3 May near a barricade erected by the police (!) on the Hermannstraße.[42]

At noon on 4 May the clashes came to an end when Zörgiebel ordered the police to use firearms only when a culprit was visible, to cease the 'indiscriminate shooting' into windows, and 'to avoid [using] excessive force'.[43] During the four days 198 people were wounded and 33 killed immediately or died later as a result of their injuries. Ten of the victims had been killed in flats or on balconies. Only one victim was a member of a Communist organisation. No policeman was among the dead. Of the forty-seven injured policemen only one was wounded by gunshot. Altogether 10,981 rounds of ammunition were fired from guns and pistols by the police. All the bullets lodged in the corpses of those killed were found by subsequent police investigations to have come from police weapons.[44] Police Commander Magnus Heimannsberg and Police Vice-President Dr. Bernhard Weiß regarded the publication of the investigation findings compiled on 4 June 1929 'as not appropriate for the time being'.[45] It appeared as if a Pandora's Box had been opened. At the bottom of this box one could have detected the ghostly outlines of the bloody suppression of the revolutionary movements at the beginning of 1919.

Explanation and Interpretation of Police Behaviour

The police's repertoire of behaviour, habits, conduct while on duty and conception the enemy during the bloody May days of 1929 in Berlin hark back to another era, quite apart from the fact that an unbiased observer might well wonder whether it was a police or military force which had been in action here. Some of the scenes described above suggest that when seeking to explain the behaviour of the police in May 1929, as so often when one wants to comprehend the problems of Weimar, one needs to look back to the early phase of the Republic.

The Prussian police in the Weimar Republic were, to put it pointedly, not a product of the revolution of 1918–19 but of the counter-revolution of 1919. For a short time after the collapse of the Wilhelmine police in November 1918, security organs of workers and soldiers defence squads (*Arbeiter- und Soldatenwehren*) formed the police. The opportunity given to the army, still at the Western Front and largely intact, by the revolutionary government to intervene in domestic politics, was taken up energetically by the Army High Command. The Spartacist Revolt, an unprepared spontaneous uprising of left-wing radical supporters of the Independent Social Democratic Party (USPD) and the newly-established KPD in the Berlin newspaper quarter in January 1919, marked the beginning of a bloody campaign against the council movement by the *Freikorps* and volunteer formations, consisting in large measure of soldiers who had returned from the front and were granted police powers by Army Minister Gustav Noske. Until the summer of 1919, the regular police played hardly any part in these military-style campaigns to disband various small 'Council-Republics' and strongholds of radical-socialist workers movements. 'Domestic order' was reestablished with field howitzers, flame throwers, hand grenades and machine guns. Massacres and arbitrary executions were not uncommon.

Following the establishment of the postrevolutionary Prussian government, the Prussian Ministry of the Interior and the Army Ministry discussed plans to rebuild of the Prussian police, and it quickly became clear that a militarised police model would be favoured. On the one hand, it was assumed that armed, radical left-wing masses and 'red armies' would remain a constant threat to internal security in future; on the other hand, the unrest in the spring of 1919, following the Spartacist Uprising in January, appeared to have demonstrated that the use of a militarised police along the lines of Noske's *Freikorps* would be successful. Beginning in May 1919 and with the support of the army, a militarily organised, uniformed and equipped police force, which encompassed 23,500 men by February 1920, was placed alongside the 37,000 constables taken over from the old police forces of the former Empire.[46] In order to set up the formations of this 'Security Police', in some cases companies and battalions from the army, in the process of being reduced in size according to the terms of the Versailles Treaty, were taken over in their entirety. The same was true for *Freikorps* and volunteer formations. The training of the Security Police was based on army regulations and infantry engagements, with exercises in camouflage, capturing terrain, house-to-house fighting, the use of hand grenades, etc. Even following the establishment of police training schools after 1921 it was not genuine police training, something which already had existed in the Empire, but the military aspects of training which continued to dominate the curriculum.

This development was due not least to the particular mentality and military approach of the men transferred from numerous *Freikorps* and army units into the new Security Police and put in leadership positions. The men who became officers, and thus leaders of police formations, as well as supervisors and instructors at the police training schools, were mainly those who previously had served as officers in the army and the *Freikorps* and had been part of the special group of 'front officers'. They were characterised by a particular approach to their lives and careers, which bore the stamp not of the experience of membership of the prewar officer corps, which had served to integrate and accustom people to hierarchies, but of the decivilised, self-sufficient life in the trenches on the Western Front. These officers tended towards a conspiratorial allegiance to their own group and oriented themselves politically in black and white categories; one thinks of the stab-in-the-back legend eagerly soaked up in these circles and the demagogic condemnation of the Social

Democratic 'November Criminals'. The experiences of long-serving police officers in their everyday duties and in the police training schools were minimal and disregarded by the new officers of the Security Police, who were able rapidly to advance their careers due to the alleged 'failure' of the police during the revolution.

Many officers of the Security Police had their own ideas about policing and did not trouble themselves over the instructions from their superiors in the police and government administration when they took their own initiative to search homes, make arrests or use police vehicles for private purposes. The political quality of the police officer corps was apparent from their defamation of both the symbols and the most prominent politicians of the Weimar Republic, not just while drinking heavily in the officers' mess but also frequently in public. Contacts by police officers with right-wing groups and secret associations were discovered in connection with the assassinations of Matthias Erzberger and Walther Rathenau. The political orientation of the majority of the Prussian police officer corps was more than apparent during the Kapp-Lüttwitz Putsch of March 1920, when virtually all the middle and higher-ranking police officers supported the putschists while the majority of the chief police officers in the Prussian provinces remained indifferent and adopted a wait-and-see attitude towards the Putsch attempt. The Social Democrat Carl Severing, appointed Prussian Interior Minister after the collapse of this attempt to overthrow the government, dismissed some of the police officers who had revealed their political unreliability during the coup, but he did not make any fundamental change in Prussian policing as it had developed from the spring of 1919. The Security Police and the former 'Order Police' (the *Schutzmänner*) were combined to form the Prussian *Schutzpolizei* encompassing 54,000 men, while the Criminal Investigation Police and the rural gendarmerie (*Landjägerei*) held a special position within the 85,000 police posts in Prussia permitted by the Allies.

The army had also proved itself disloyal to the republican political order during the Kapp-Lüttwitz Putsch, and Severing's concern above all was to remove its role as regulator of domestic political crisis and the holder of executive power during the many states of emergency ordered by the Reich President during the early years of the Weimar Republic. As Prussia's militarily organised and led executive force, the new *Schutzpolizei* was supposed to deal with further expected mass uprising attempts by right and left against the Republic, as well as to block the expansion of the power of the army in domestic politics.

In Severing's eyes proof of the correctness of this basic orientation of Prussian police policy under Social Democratic leadership had been provided by the deployment of the *Schutzpolizei* during the attempted uprising by the KPD in the Prussian province of Saxony in March 1921. The KPD provoked an uprising in the central German industrial region around Halle and Merseburg, which had been unsettled since the revolutionary days of 1918–19 and which was home to the huge industrial complex at Leuna. This was meant to demonstrate to German workers the revolutionary élan of the Party, whose membership had grown substantially since it combined with the USPD in 1920, and to sweep along the workers in other German industrial regions towards the desired great revolution. More and more *Schutzpolizei* units were transferred into the region, which had been shaken by strikes and looting. The Communist adventurer Max Hoelz gathered hundreds of followers, ready for action, and sought confrontations with the Prussian *Schutzpolizei*. On 23 March 1921 the first bloody incident occurred. Small mobile contingents of well-motivated workers, most of them from the immediate area, received effective machine gun cover from Hoelz's troops who, from their positions on hills and slag heaps, were able to control the entire vicinity without themselves offering a target for light weapons. Twenty *Schutzpolizisten* were attacked in this manner on the grounds of a mine near Eisleben; four died in a hail of bullets, five more were wounded.[47]

The clashes dragged on in the form of a small-scale war of constant movement until 29 March, the day when the last stronghold of the revolutionaries, the fortified Leuna factory, was captured. Four thousand Prussian police had faced 3–4 thousand revolutionary fighters; 35 members of the police and 145 civilians were killed. Both sides were guilty of the massacre of prisoners and of torture, although the main culprits in this regard were the police during and immediately after the fighting. With the support of Reich President Friedrich Ebert, Severing was able to fend off the constant pressure of the army leadership to let their troops be deployed to suppress the uprising. In the event the involvement of the army was limited to providing an artillery battery which 'softened up' the factory grounds before police formations stormed the Leuna works on the morning of 29 March.

The measures taken by Police Colonel Bernhard Graf von Poninski, the commander of the operation, including the systematic shooting and maltreatment of prisoners, were covered up by Severing. An offer of amnesty and negotiations, which a police major made to the rebels in Eisleben on 25 March, was rejected by Severing with the comment: 'Ruthless measures are to be taken against the rebels and no leniency is to be permitted.'[48] A few years later Police Colonel von Poninski became head of the largest Prussian police training school, in Brandenburg an der Havel, which sent 320 of its students to participate in the 'battles' in Berlin during the Blood May of 1929.[49]

Prussian interior minister Severing judged the success of the Prussian *Schutzpolizei* in suppressing the March 1921 uprising as a confirmation of his policing policy. The main element of the Prussian police reform after 1919, concentrating the *Schutzpolizei* into powerful units organised along military lines, was retained and embedded in the training of the police. There was hardly any space left for the development of new ideas along the lines of a civilian police. The events of the Hamburg October uprising of 1923 also seemed to confirm this policy, as the action of the police at that time was not accompanied to the same extent by ugly outbursts of violence as during the 1921 uprising in central Germany.

The disquieting and damaging developments within the police officer corps, which became clear not only by the manner in which officers behaved during the 1921 uprising, were not fundamentally opposed by Severing. Admittedly Severing's hands would have been tied by civil-service law and its regulation of the police officer's career, had he attempted energetically to achieve the speedy dismissal of some police officers through the disciplinary procedures. However, it appears much more likely that here, as in other areas of policy, the decisive role was played by the political lethargy of Severing himself, who admitted that he had nothing against working with monarchist civil servants, and also by the authoritarian bent of the leading Social Democrats in Prussia (Severing, Braun, Grzesinski) as opposed to the prominent Social Democrats at Reich level; they had an inclination to behave as representatives of the state and took pleasure in military pageantry.

The Prussian police officer corps, which displayed considerable homogeneity in the ages and mental outlooks of its personnel, as a consequence of the large increases in recruitment in 1919–20, and whose leaders until the end of the Weimar Republic were almost entirely veterans of the First World War, had almost free range after 1921 to implement its policing policy. The 1921 uprising, also referred to as the 'March Action', and its suppression by the police, now became the point of reference and benchmark for all police training insofar as it involved so-called 'large-scale deployment', that is the concerted deployment of major police formations. Obviously it was almost exclusively the Communists who were assumed to be the 'enemy' in police exercises and manoeuvres. Police constables, and particularly the candidates at the Prussian police training schools, were initiated into 'the strict discipline of firearms training'; they practised 'advancing into built-up areas under cover of firearms', movement 'in closed and open formation using cover against being seen and fired upon', 'target practice', 'judging distances and map-reading', and 'orienting themselves by day and night'. A high ranking police officer summed up his policing expertise with the words: 'Too forceful a bearing can be a mistake. However, too weak a bearing is a bigger mistake.' And one of his colleagues left no doubt that in the case of unrest 'the opportune use of firearms right at the beginning' would 'nip it in the bud'.[50] During 1927, for example, the journal *Die Polizei* published a series of articles written by police officers drawing lessons from the combat experiences of the early phase of the Republic for police actions in large cities. The armour-plated 'special vehicle' was regarded as especially useful for providing 'mobile covering fire for advancing assault troops, especially for clearing out barricades or for raking a cross street with gunfire'. As soon as a 'district is taken, the so-called pacification begins'.[51] The exercise 'Armed uprising. Police deployed to restore order' included: 'Brisk gunfire from the rooftops and from the upper floors. Street barricaded and occupied'. Added to this was the instruction to inform the inhabitants that they had to close their windows: 'Any open window will be fired upon ruthlessly.'[52]

The readiness to use force and the entirely inappropriate behaviour of the police during the confrontations in Berlin during May 1929 can be traced back to groundwork which had been laid over many years and to a fatal narrowing of perspective at all levels of the Prussian police force. It appears that the police involved in the Blood May conjured up German soldiers' images of the terrorist 'Franktireur' in occupied Belgium during the First World War,[53] images of Spartacists shooting from behind barricades of newspaper rolls in January 1919, and images of Communist machine-gunners on the slag-heaps of Eisleben during March 1921. It did not really matter whether or not the individual police constable had actually experienced these scenes at first hand. Right up to the end of the Blood May no police officer deployed in Wedding or Neukölln seems to have realised that he was fighting not a Communist uprising but a phantom.

The conclusion which the Association of Prussian Police Officers drew from the debacle in Berlin in May 1929 was clear: something was very wrong with the training of the police, for the 'May Unrest' proved that it had 'gone short' of training with firearms.[54] For the writer Karl Kraus the Berlin events in May 1929 left the impression that the difference between the Monarchy and the Republic lay solely in 'that today the ground where no grass grows is occupied by the police rather than the military'.[55]

(translated by Richard Bessel and Sabine Phillips)

Notes

1. Klaus-Michael Mallmann, *Kommunisten in der Weimarer Republik. Sozialgeschichte einer revolutionären Bewegung* (Darmstadt, 1996).
2. Mallmann, *Kommunisten in der Weimarer Republik*, p. 360.
3. Hermann Weber, *Die Wandlung des deutschen Kommunismus. Die Stalinisierung der KPD in der Weimarer Republik* (Frankfurt am Main, 1969), vol. 1, p. 224.
4. Heinrich August Winkler, *Der Schein der Normalität. Arbeiter und Arbeiterbewegung in der Weimarer Republik 1924 bis 1930* (Berlin and Bonn, 1985), p. 679.
5. Ossip K. Flechtheim, *Die KPD in der Weimarer Republik* (Frankfurt am Main, 1969), p. 257.
6. Arthur Rosenberg, *Geschichte der Weimarer Republik* (Frankfurt am Main, 1975), p. 199.
7. Thomas Kurz, 'Arbeitermörder und Putschisten. Der Berliner "Blutmai" von 1929 als Kristallisationspunkt des Verhältnisses von KPD und SPD vor der Katastrophe', *Internationale Wissenschaftliche Korrespondenz* 22 (1986), pp. 297–317 (here p. 309); Léon Schirmann, *Blutmai Berlin 1929. Dichtungen und Wahrheit* (Berlin 1991), p. 66ff.
8. Schirmann, *Blutmai Berlin 1929*, p. 292f.
9. Chris Bowlby, 'Blutmai 1929: Police, Parties and Proletarians in a Berlin Confrontation', *Historical Journal* 24 (1986), pp. 137–58 (here 152ff); Mallmann, *Kommunisten in der Weimarer Republik*, p. 196f.
10. Hans-Peter Ehni, *Bollwerk Preußen? Preußen-Regierung, Reich-Länder-Problem und Sozialdemokratie 1928–1932* (Bonn, 1975), p. 150f.
11. Ehni, *Bollwerk Preußen?* p. 151.
12. Peter Leßmann, *Die preußische Schutzpolizei in der Weimarer Republik. Streifendienst und Straßenkampf* (Düsseldorf, 1989), p. 274f.
13. Thomas Kurz, *'Blutmai'. Sozialdemokraten und Kommunisten im Brennpunkt der Berliner Ereignisse von 1929* (Berlin and Bonn 1988), p. 109.
14. Anthony Glees, 'Albert C. Grzesinski and the Politics of Prussia, 1926–1930', *English Historical Review* 90 (1974), pp. 814–34 (here 832).
15. Dietrich Orlow, 'Preußen und der Kapp-Putsch', *Vierteljahrshefte für Zeitgeschichte*, 26 (1978), pp. 191–236; Eberhard Kolb, *Die Weimarer Republik* (Munich, 1993), p. 221.

Peter Leßmann-Faust

16. Ehni, *Bollwerk Preußen?* p. 151: 'The immediate motive for the senseless violent action against harmless demonstrators remains unknown.' Winkler, *Der Schein der Normalität*, p. 673: 'It is not sufficient to explain the behaviour of the police by the hatred with which the forces of order were met in the working-class neighbourhoods, not even by the only too understandable fear of communist crossfire. A considerable share of the responsibility lay with the Berlin Police President.'

17. Polizei-Oberst a.D. Hans Lange, in *Die Menschenrechte* (published by the Deutsche Liga für Menschenrechte), vol. 4 (1929), Appendix 1 to 'Die Ergebnisse der Maiuntersuchung', pp. 9ff.

18. Kurt G. Schuster, *Der Rote Frontkämpfer-Bund 1924–29* (Düsseldorf, 1975), p. 19f.

19. Eve Rosenhaft, 'Gewalt in Politik. Zum Problem des sozialen Militarismus', in Klaus Jürgen Müller and Eckart Opitz (eds.), *Militär und Militarismus in der Weimarer Republik* (Düsseldorf, 1978), pp. 237–59 (here: pp. 243, 251ff).

20. Mallmann, *Kommunisten in der Weimarer Republik*, p. 193.

21. Mallmann, *Kommunisten in der Weimarer Republik*, p. 195.

22. Leßmann, *Die preußische Schutzpolizei*, p. 266f.

23. Schuster, *Der Rote Frontkämpfer-Bund*, pp. 193–224.

24. Hermann Weber, *Hauptfeind Sozialdemokratie. Strategie und Taktik der KPD 1929–1933* (Düsseldorf, 1982).

25. Carl Severing, *Mein Lebensweg* (Cologne, 1950), vol. 2, p. 141.

26. Schirmann, *Blutmai Berlin 1929*, pp. 45, 53f.

27. Schuster, *Der Rote Frontkämpfer-Bund*, pp. 213ff; Ehni, *Bollwerk Preußen?* p. 159f.

28. Severing, *Mein Lebensweg*, p. 187.

29. Schuster, *Der Rote Frontkämpfer-Bund*, p. 217f.

30. Leßmann, *Die preußische Schutzpolizei*, p. 270.

31. Hsi-Huey Liang, *Die Berliner Polizei in der Weimarer Republik* (Berlin and New York, 1977), p. 120.

32. Unless otherwise stated, descriptions here of the events in Berlin from 1 to 4 May 1929 are based on the following sources: 'Authentischer Bericht über den Berliner Polizeikrieg', *Das Tagebuch* 9 (1929), pp. 771–9: 'Die Ergebnisse der Maiuntersuchung', in Deutsche Liga für Menschenrechte (ed.), *Die Menschenrechte*, (1929) vol. 4, pp. 1–8; *Die Weltbühne* 25 (1929), pp. 729–36. In addition, see Eve Rosenhaft, 'Working-Class Life and Working-Class Politics. Communists, Nazis and the State in the Battle for the Streets, Berlin 1928–1932', in Richard Bessel and E.J. Feuchtwanger (eds.), *Social Change and Political Development in Weimar Germany* (London and Totowa, New Jersey, 1981), pp. 207–40 (here pp. 227ff); Bowlby, 'Blutmai 1929', passim; Kurz, *'Blutmai'*, pp. 28–68; Schirmann, *Blutmai Berlin 1929*, pp. 82–166.

33. Here especially Kurz, *'Blutmai'*, pp. 38ff. Compare Schirmann, *Blutmai Berlin 1929*, p. 124f.

34. Quoted in Schirmann, *Blutmai Berlin 1929*, p. 123.

35. Leßmann, *Die preußische Schutzpolizei*, p. 272.

36. Quoted in Schirmann, *Blutmai Berlin 1929*, p.123.

37. Liang, *Die Berliner Polizei*, p. 121. See Schirmann, *Blutmai Berlin 1929*, p. 146f.

38. Schirmann, *Blutmai Berlin 1929*, p. 156f.

39. Schirmann, *Blutmai Berlin 1929*, p. 157f; Bowlby, 'Blutmai 1929', p. 145; Kurz, *'Blutmai'*, p. 43.

40. Schirmann, *Blutmai Berlin 1929*, p. 140.

41. Figures and quotation from Schirmann, *Blutmai Berlin 1929*, p. 152f.
42. Reference and quotation from Schirmann, *Blutmai Berlin 1929*, pp. 153–66; Leßmann, *Die preußische Schutzpolizei*, p. 273.
43. Leßmann, *Die preußische Schutzpolizei*, p. 167. Quotations from Kurz, '*Blutmai*', p. 67. In the most recent investigation of the Blood May, Leon Schirmann puts forward, in greater detail than Ehni did previously (Ehni, *Bollwerk Preußen?* p. 153), the thesis that Grzesinski deliberately let the police intervene harshly on 3 May, so that he could convince Prussian Prime Minister Braun and the Reich Interior Minister Severing, at a meeting which began that morning at 11 o'clock, of the need to ban the RFB. One of the items on the agenda was 'the dissolution of Communist organisations'. In particular Grzesinski had to convince Severing, who was opposed to banning the RFB. In the event, Severing conceded: The RFB was banned on 6 May in Prussia and on 10 May 1929 throughout Germany. See Schirmann, *Blutmai Berlin 1929*, pp. 152f, 161f, 279–82; Leßmann, *Die preußische Schutzpolizei*, p. 278.
44. Leßmann, *Die preußische Schutzpolizei*, p. 274; Schirmann, p. 83.
45. Quotation from Leßmann, *Die preußische Schutzpolizei*, p. 274.
46. Statistics and all further information here and the following pages, from Leßmann, *Die preußische Schutzpolizei*, pp. 17–119, 222–51.
47. Christian Knatz, 'Ein Durchbruch mit militärischem Einschlag – Die preußische Schutzpolizei und der Mitteldeutsche Aufstand von 1921', *Archiv für Polizeigeschichte*, 7 (1996), pp. 75–91 (here p. 79).
48. Knatz, 'Ein Durchbruch mit militärischem Einschlag', pp. 81f, 86f.
49. Knatz, 'Ein Durchbruch mit militärischem Einschlag', p. 87; Schirmann, *Blutmai Berlin 1929*, p. 77.
50. Quotations from textbooks and training plans from Leßmann, *Die preußische Schutzpolizei*, pp. 241–7.
51. Quotation from Kurz, '*Blutmai*', p. 75.
52. Quotation from Schirmann, *Blutmai Berlin 1929*, p. 49.
53. Schirmann, *Blutmai Berlin 1929*, p. 93.
54. Quotation from Leßmann, *Die preußische Schutzpolizei*, p. 275.
55. Karl Kraus, *Schriften*, Christian Wagenknecht (ed.), (Frankfurt am Main, 1993), vol. 18, p. 64 (from an essay by Kraus with the title: 'Vom Zörgiebel. Ein Kapitel vom Gutem Geschmack').

2

The police and the Clichy Massacre, March 1937

Simon Kitson

As the *journées* of the revolutionary period, disorders throughout the nineteenth century, in the 1920s and 1930s and more recently in May 1968 testify, the 'street' has traditionally represented a source of danger for French political regimes. The weight of this tradition developed into something of a paranoia for governments which have felt the need to control tightly and supervise this public arena. For Republican regimes the emphasis on order has been complicated by their proclaimed attachment to the notion of liberty, but even they tended to give greater priority to maintaining public order than to catering for the freedom to demonstrate. They did not hesitate to draw on repressive legislation or to issue firm instructions to the forces of law and order. The police, the gendarmerie and the army – the three bodies used to implement this policy – acquired a deserved reputation for ferocity and brutality, and were frequently criticised for lashing out at innocent by-standers.

In the mid-1930s a new government was elected which many hoped would have a less brutal approach to public order issues.[1] The Popular Front, led by Socialists and Radicals with support from Communists, civil rights' movements and leading trade unions, came to power in June 1936 under the premiership of Léon Blum. This coalition was born in the aftermath of the extreme right-wing riots of 6 February 1934, during which fifteen people died and several hundred were injured, and which had appeared to threaten France's system of parliamentary democracy. In these circumstances it is little wonder that the ability to maintain public order remained of basic importance for France's new leaders and was considered as a fundamental source of legitimacy. Even the Communists had fought the 1936 election campaign as the defenders of public order. The Socialists for their part promised a new conception of order. They declared that a successful policy in this respect was dependent on a new relationship between the government and the population, with the former serving as a mediator between employers and employees, giving itself the mission of preserving social harmony. However, they were not naive enough to believe that they could bypass the need for a loyal police force. No sooner had the Popular Front arrived in office than it began increasing police wages and manpower whilst announcing its determination to purge political opponents from the hierarchy of this administration.[2]

The promised social harmony seemed rapidly to have materialised that summer as the government and the unions, using the large-scale strikes and occupation of factories that followed the elections, wrung major concessions from the employers, including paid holidays and a reduction of the working week. The Minister of the Interior, Roger Salengro, refused to send the police to displace striking workers and could proudly announce that the largest social disturbances in French history were ended with no bloodshed. However, the situation rapidly turned sour for the government. Salengro committed suicide in November following a scandalous extreme-right newspaper campaign. The failure of Blum to intervene openly in the Spanish Civil War was resented by much of the working class who saw this non-intervention as a betrayal of everything for which the Popular Front stood. Economic difficulties loomed large. Investors boycotted the French economy. Meanwhile, the Defence Minister Edouard Daladier announced an increase of 47 percent in defence expenditure for the 1937 budget, placing a heavy burden on the already overstretched government finances and forcing other ministers to look for cuts in expenditure. Suspicions that the government was betraying the hopes of its electorate gained credibility when, on 13 February 1937, Léon Blum announced the necessity of a pause in the government's social programme.[3]

This pause further undermined the government. Not only did it cause Popular Front militants to cast suspicious eyes on their leaders but for the right-wing opposition it represented a sign of weakness, hinting that the moment was right to act. Despite the irresistible momentum of the Popular Front in the May 1936 elections it should not be assumed that the opposition had been silenced on a long-term basis. In winning the election the Left had obtained only a relatively small increase in votes (less than 300,000) since the 1932 elections. The dynamism of its victory had come from the level of engagement rather than the number of its electors, with traditional radical voters shifting leftwards to the socialists and some traditional socialists switching to the communists. But the sizeable right-wing electorate (36 percent of registered voters) had also radicalized. The *Croix de Feu*, which now changed its name to *Parti Social Français* (PSF), in an attempt to present itself as a respectable and legal political party, was the principal beneficiary of this movement in right-wing sensibilities. Even if its opponents accused it of being a camouflaged fascist league, the PSF became the fastest growing party in the year following the elections.[4]

It was the PSF decision to hold a meeting in the town of Clichy on 16 March which provided the venue for an explosion of violence which would underline both the frustration of the left and the radicalisation of the right. This meeting could not really be described as a political rally: it was rather a family gathering of PSF supporters, grouping together 400 men and 80 women and children in the Olympia cinema for the showing of the screen adaptation of Claude Farrère's book *La Bataille.*[5] Rumour spread that the PSF's national leader, Colonel de la Roque, was to attend the meeting in person. That this event was seen as such a provocation owed much to the political colour of the town. Part of the red belt around Paris, Clichy was a suburb divided between two left-wing currents: the National Assembly deputy, Maurice Honel, was a Communist; the mayor, Charles Auffray, was a former Communist now wearing Socialist colours, whilst the Conseiller Général, Maurice Naile, had oscillated between the two formations before finally settling with the Communists. Hostility to the PSF was further engendered by recent attempts by some local employers, seen as sympathetic to this movement, to institute 'scab' trade unions and to expel members of the left-wing union the CGT (*Confédération Générale de Travail*) from Clichy's factories. Neither could anyone in Clichy have forgotten the recent death in the town of an Algerian worker shot by his PSF employer.[6]

The local Popular Front committee's request to have the PSF gathering banned was rejected by the Interior Ministry, which justified the decision by reference to freedom of assembly. After all, the PSF was still officially a legal political party; although the government had begun proceedings against its leaders – on the grounds that they were seeking to reconstitute a fascist-style league of the type outlawed by the decrees of 18 and 23 June 1936 – it was not until 1 March 1937 that the dossier was passed to the relevant section of the courts. Failing to get the PSF gathering forbidden, the Left decided to organize a simultaneous counter-demonstration. Since 1934, demonstrations designed to show the cohesion and strength of the forces defending democracy had formed an essential part of anti-fascist strategy. The organizers of the counter-demonstration were keen to avoid any excesses. So, on the eve of their march, they carefully hammered out the details regarding the route and the precautions to be taken with police officials. They agreed that at no point should they come into direct contact with the PSF militants and that they would avoid the rue de l'Union where the Olympia was situated, limiting themselves instead to assembling in front of the town hall, which, as bad luck would have it, was situated in close proximity to the cinema.[7]

On 16 March 1937, the police faced a predicament similar to that which they encountered several times a week: both the gathering and the counter-demonstration were legal and hence both had to be protected and supervised. The strategy adopted by the police was to establish, at a distance from the cinema, fixed roadblocks designed to keep the two groups apart. As was usual, the technical aspects of the police preparations were organised by a *Commissaire Divisionaire* (Chief Superintendent), in this case *Commissaire* Poirson, the forty-nine-year-old head of Paris's municipal police force. The local Clichy policemen were reinforced with detachments from the Paris police as well as from the *garde mobile* and *garde républicaine*; the latter both formed part of the gendarmerie and hence enjoyed a special half-military, half-police status. A total police presence of 1,583 men had been planned comprising 324 uniformed *gardiens de la paix* on foot or on bicycle, 34 plain-clothed officers, 1,200 *gardes mobiles* and 25 mounted *gardes républicaines*. The police officers were to occupy the front row of the roadblocks so as to form a buffer between the demonstrators and the *gardes mobiles*; given the military origin of the *gardes mobiles* it was considered a provocation to bring them into direct contact with the crowd. To avoid any incident the police began their surveillance around the Olympia at nine o'clock in the morning, reinforcing it in the afternoon since rumours were rife that a left-wing sit-in would be staged in the cinema to prevent the PSF gathering. It seemed that all the necessary precautions had been taken to assure that the day passed off as peacefully as possible.[8]

That afternoon left-wing demonstrators started arriving from neighbouring communes; the numbers were to reach a peak of somewhere between 6,000 and 10,000 that evening. The crowd was in a highly excitable mood and it was at 6.10 p.m. that the first incidents were noted. Around 500 demonstrators attempted to force their way into the cinema in the rue de l'Union. The police pushed them back. However, after consultation with the deputy, Honel, and the mayor, Auffray, they decided that it would be seen as a provocation to force the demonstrators to evacuate the rue de l'Union altogether. Both Honel and Auffray addressed the demonstrators, calling for calm, but to no avail because their speeches were lost in the noise of the crowd. Scarcely ten metres wide the rue de l'Union was too narrow for so many people. Pushing began. Around 8.10 p.m. skirmishes began between police and demonstrators as the latter tried to force through roadblocks. This escalation of violence compelled *Commissaire* Poirson to send for reinforcements from Paris at 9.00 p.m. and to order the evacuation of the cinema by a back entrance at 9.15 p.m. Shortly afterwards the first shots were fired, although it is not clear who fired them or why. The demonstrators claimed that the police had been the first to use arms, whilst the police claimed that the initial shots were fired from the crowd. Objects were thrown at the police and a plain-clothed police officer, Louis Daguet, was later to produce his hat through which a bullet had passed during these initial incidents.[9]

It was the appearance of the reinforcements from Paris between 9.25 p.m. and 9.45 p.m. that caused the trouble to escalate. Police vans arrived individually in an uncoordinated fashion and quickly found themselves in the midst of a hostile crowd who viewed their arrival as a provocation. Some officers tried to pacify the crowd. The police *brigadier,* Georges Houzelle, climbed onto the bonnet of his police van and appealed for calm. About ten demonstrators stepped forward to lend weight to his request. However, just when Houzelle was convinced of his success, a surge of demonstrators pushed forward, throwing punches and even lashing out at their more pacific fellow demonstrators. But most officers arriving on the scene were not offered the chance of proving their prowess as public speakers. Abuse was hurled at them; paving stones, spikes from railings, indeed anything which came to hand rained down on them and even some shots were fired in their direction from the street and surrounding buildings. One demonstrator climbed on to the running board of a police vehicle, placed a gun under the chin of *Sousbrigadier* Achille Besnard and fired upwards, grazing the side of his face. Of the 25 occupants in one of the first police vans to arrive, twenty-two were injured even before alighting from their vehicle. It was at this moment that most of the casualties were inflicted, as some police officers clearly used their weapons on their attackers.[10]

Calm mysteriously returned more rapidly than the violence had flared up. *Commissaire* Poirson was mystified to explain this sudden pacification but suggested it might be linked to a number of arrests and to the sight of the wounded and dead. No sooner had the violence subsided than a battle of statistics began to try to establish which side had more casualties and hence by implication where responsibility for the incidents must lie. All of the dead were from amongst the demonstrators, hit by bullets from Browning 7.65 mm revolvers: standard police issue. Five communists – René Chrétien, Emile Mahé, Victor Magermann, Arthur Lepers and Marcel Cerruti – were killed outright, whilst a thirty-nine-year-old Socialist militant, Solange Demangel, was to die on 1 May from the bullet she received in the head at Clichy. Estimates at the number of wounded varied considerably between different sources ranging from 80 to 500 for the demonstrators side and from 137 to 242 for the police side. André Blumel, Blum's principal private secretary, was amongst the wounded, as were local politicians *Conseiller-Général* Naile and Mayor Auffray.[11]

Much blame was apportioned to the police. One analysis was that the police had been keen to settle political scores with the Left. It was said that Jean Chiappe, the former Prefect of Police, a person of extreme-right wing persuasion whose dismissal had played a role in the riots of February 1934, had maintained a large reservoir of supporters in the Paris police. Even though the Parisian force also contained important radical and socialist currents, there were undoubtedly still a number of police officers devoted to Chiappe. Whether or not one believes the witness who claimed that *Brigadier* Georges Henriroux of the Eighth Paris *arrondissement* had boasted in a bar of having fired bullets at Clichy and had regretted that there were not 10,000 deaths amongst the demonstrators, anti-communism certainly was strongly implanted at all levels of the police.

However, to attribute police behaviour that day solely to political considerations is probably an oversimplification. Police violence against demonstrators had become embroidered into their professional culture. After hours of waiting for something to happen during demonstrations, bored police officers had developed the habit of lashing out at demonstrators in a display of virility to assure respect in the mainly masculine world of street demonstrations. That at Clichy this violence escalated was explained partly by the attitude of the demonstrators, but also by strategic and human considerations on the police side. The organisers of the counter-demonstration had failed to keep control of their troops, who were in turn frustrated and angry at government compromises, of which the failure to ban the PSF gathering was the latest example. The danger for the Popular Front was that, spearheading a movement which encouraged the citizen's involvement in politics, this involvement might turn against government representatives when the public mood turned sour – as the police now discovered. Tactical incompetence caused the police reaction to be inappropriate. The intermittent arrival of isolated police vans in the midst of a riot, with vague instructions and no hierarchical control (as luck would have it the officer who was supposed to command these reinforcements was injured in the first van), suggests that the police responded in a fashion resonant with human frailty. Faced with the hostility of the crowd and their inability to overpower demonstrators by more traditional means the police lost their composure and resorted to the use of their weapons out of concerns for self-preservation.[12]

Some historians have argued that underlying these issues there was also a successful provocation by forces of the extreme right, which had managed to place *agents provocateurs* in the ranks of both the demonstrators and the police. There is a modicum of evidence to support such an argument and the preceeding discussion certainly does not discount such a possibility. *Gardien de la paix* Joseph Bourgeois overheard a group of individuals discussing their plans to disrupt the Left's demonstration and 'to smash the face in of the reds and if necessary of the police'. The Socialist General Councillor Jean Longuet claimed that amongst those arrested was an individual found to be carrying both Communist and PSF membership cards. According to the Socialist Jules Moch, one of the casualties was recognised as a 'provocateur' frequently operating in the north of France, whilst some unknown demonstrators were later identified as members of the anti-republican Cagoule movement, to whom some historians have attributed the first shots. If this was a provocation it was perfectly in keeping with the tactics deployed by the Cagoule in their attempt to subvert the Republic since their clandestine foundation in 1936 by former militants of the far-right *Action Française*.[13]

Whatever the truth, Clichy did untold damage to the reputation of both the Popular Front and the police. In Parliament, Léon Blum took to the podium to criticise police excesses whilst insisting that the police were the 'sons of the people'. Other socialists echoed the same theme, underlining that the vast majority of police personnel were solid republicans but admitting the presence of some 'Chiappistes' in the force. Communists, such as the municipal councillor Georges Marrane, stressed that Clichy compromised the good relationship that had been established between the police and workers since the advent of the Popular Front and argued that the political purge of the police needed to go much deeper, since the fascists continued to benefit from a certain level of complicity in the institution. The main body of the Left officially stood by the government. In a vote of confidence following these incidents the executive obtained 362 votes against 215; throughout the country Popular Front committees declared their continued loyalty, whilst the unions called for a strike in Paris on 18 March to 'defend public order' and, as their leaders explained, to direct public anger away from the government. However, behind these shows of support relations were strained. The Communists, who started to attach the epithet of 'assassin' to Blum, called for the resignation of the Interior Minister Marx Dormoy. The revolutionary left of the Socialist party issued tracts asking whether state violence against anti-fascist workers was the price the government had agreed to pay for the confidence of the banks, to which the Socialist leadership responded by insisting on the dissolution of this faction. As the unity of the Left wavered, the Right revelled in the situation arguing that the Popular Front had lost control of both the police and the workers and declaring that what had happened at Clichy was an attempted Communist revolution. Blum's government staggered on for another three months, but public order issues had once again revealed their crucial importance in political stability.[14]

Perhaps the most striking paradox of the Clichy affair was that both the police and the demonstrators believed that they had prepared the event so thoroughly that no violence would occur. In keeping with the conciliatory spirit of the times a dialogue had been established between representatives of the police and the organisers of the demonstration to hammer out details beforehand. But however well prepared they were for a well-ordered counter demonstration, all police contingency plans were wrecked by an inability to cope once events had started to diverge from the intended route. As it turned out, communications between the police and the militants beyond the organisers were problematic. Although the Popular Front had been marked by a thawing of relations between the police and the extreme left, street fights between the two were too recent for either side to have forgotten, and both groups undoubtedly brought a preconceived stereotype of the other with them to Clichy. The fragility of their détente was shown by the rapidity with which the encounter degenerated into violence. Whatever the truth of manipulation by the Cagoule, the success of sinister provocations of this type depend on the readiness of the protagonists to be provoked.

As so often happens with such tragedies, all sides made subsequent attempts to recast the incident and use it for their own ends. The right and the extreme right played on the divisions between the component parts of the government. The extreme left tried to use it to put pressure on the government not to compromise on its principles. Marx Dormoy, the interior minister, took advantage of the occasion to step up his campaign against the extreme right, and ultimately succeeded in dismantling much of the Cagoule organisation later that year. In order to assess more clearly what the Cagoule was planning, in April 1937 he proposed, in a letter to the president, the creation of a national *Direction des Renseignements Généraux* to reinforce and coordinate political policing. In 1941 Dormoy paid dearly for his success; he was assassinated by former Cagoulards. The Prefect of Police sought to profit from the Clichy affair by demanding more resources. In a press conference at the end of March he envisaged 'confronting a nervous crowd, not with the chests of men whose uniform could not remove their emotions, but rather with a mechanism against which [the crowd's] momentum would break without the shedding of blood.' Practically this meant the introduction of new technology (water cannon and tear gas) to compensate for human frailty, but he also insisted upon an expansion of the junior ranks of the police.

In the event the police, who clearly were not beyond reproach, were the only real beneficiaries of Clichy since, although their reputation was temporarily tarnished, they successfully turned the outcome to their advantage. But neither the subsequent expansion of political policing, thanks to Marx Dormoy, nor the new technologies successfully negotiated by the Prefect, prevented future demonstrations from degenerating into violence or eradicated police error. The massacre of Algerian demonstrators in Paris on 17 October 1961 and the harsh repression of communists demonstrators at Charonne on 8 February 1962 bear witness to this. Ultimately it must be asked to what extent, in moments of heightened political tension, codes of professionalism can overcome the inclination to lash out at groups or individuals that policemen consider to be dangerous.[15]

Notes

1. Jean-Marc Berlière, *Le Monde des Polices en France* (Brussels, 1996), pp. 115–32; idem, 'Du maintien de l'ordre républicain au maintien républicain de l'ordre? Réflexions sur la violence,' *Genèses* 12 (1993) pp. 6–29; idem, 'L'ordre et la sécurité: les nouveaux corps de police mis en place par la IIIe République,' *XXe Siècle* 39 (1993) pp. 23–37; Patrick Bruneteaux, *Maintenir l'ordre. Les transformations de la violence d'Etat en régime démocratique* (Paris, 1996); Jean-Charles Jauffret, 'Armée et pouvoir politique. La question des troupes spéciales chargés du maintien de l'ordre de 1871 à 1914,' *Revue Historique* 547 (1983) pp. 97–144; Lucien Mandeville, Jean-Louis Loubet del Bayle & André Picard, 'Les forces de maintien de l'ordre en France,' *Revue de défense nationale* (1977) pp. 59–76; Jean Bedier, *Le maintien de l'ordre public* (Paris, 1938); Pierre Favre, *La manifestation* (Paris, 1990); Danielle Tartakowsky, *Les manifestations de rue en France, 1918–1968* (Paris, 1996).

2. On this question see Simon Kitson, *The Marseille Police in their Context, from Popular Front to Liberation*, D.Phil dissertation (University of Sussex, 1995), chapter one; idem, 'Les policiers marseillais et le Front Populaire,' *Vingtieme Siècle* 65 (2000) pp. 47–57; Jean Lacouture, *Léon Blum*, (Paris, 1977), p. 287; the evidence presented by Léon Blum at the Riom trial, quoted by Guy Mollet, *L'action des socialistes en 1936* (Arras, 1953) p. 7; Jean-Paul Brunet, *Histoire du Front Populaire, 1934–38* (Paris, 1991), pp. 10–20; Georges Carrot, *Le maintien de l'ordre en France au XXè Siècle* (Paris, 1990), pp. 73–90; J-P Brunet, 'Le Front Populaire', in J-F Sirinelli, *Dictionnaire Historique de la Vie Politique Française au XXè Siècle* (Paris, 1995), p. 414; Patrick H. Hutton (ed.), *Historical Dictionary of the Third French Republic, 1870–1940* (New York), p. 791; Philippe Bourdrel, *La Cagoule, 30 ans de complots* (Paris, 1970), p. 36; Jan A. Stevenson, *The Cagoule Conspiracy*, thesis for bachelor's degree (Yale University, 1972), p. 3; declarations of Roger Salengro, *Journal Officiel, Chambre des Députés*, 1st session of 26 June 1936, p. 1607; 'Du nouveau!', *L'Etatiste, Organe officiel du Syndicat National des Polices d'Etat* 86 (June 1936), p. 1; '1936,' *Le Petit Provençal*, 1 January 1936, p. 2; André Varin, 'Le Front Populaire à mis au point son programme immédiat,' *Le Petit Provençal*, 10 January 1936, p. 7.

3. Danielle Tartakowsky and Claude Willard, *Des lendemains qui chantent? La France des années folles et du Front Populaire* (Paris, 1986), p. 236; Dominique Borne and Henri Dubief, *La crise des années trente, 1929–1938* (Paris, 1989), p. 183.

4. Pierre Renouvin and René Remond (ed.), *Léon Blum, chef de gouvernement, 1936–1937* (Paris, 1981), pp. 137–159; Philippe Rudaux, *Les Croix-de-Feu et le P.S.F.* (Paris, 1967); Michael Seidman, *Workers Against Work: Labor in Paris and Barcelona during the Popular Fronts* (Berkeley, California, 1991), p. 296; Alexandre Zevaes, *Clichy en Deuil* (Paris, 1937), p. 7; Declaration of the Socialist general councillor, Jean Longuet, minutes of the session of the Conseil Général de la Seine, 17 March 1937 in *Bulletin Officiel de la Ville de Paris* (21 March 1937).

5. Archives de la Préfecture de Police de Paris (henceforth APP), BA 1648, Commissaire Divisionnaire Poirson to M the Prefect of Police, 17 March 1937; declarations of Jacques Romazotti, minutes of the session of the Conseil Général de la Seine, 17 March 1937, in *Bulletin Officiel de la Ville de Paris* (21 March 1937); Tartakowsky & Willard, *Des lendemains qui chantent?* p. 236; Jean-Paul Brunet, *Histoire du Front Populaire*, p. 82; Jules Moch, *Le Front Populaire, Grande Espérance* (Paris, 1971), p. 221; Alexandre Zevaes, *Clichy en Deuil*, p. 10.

6. Minutes of the session of the Conseil Général de la Seine, 17 March 1937 in *Bulletin Officiel de la Ville de Paris* (21 March 1937); Dominique Borne & Henri Dubief, *La crise des années trente, 1929–1938* (Paris, 1989), p. 183; Jacques Kergoat, *La France du Front Populaire, La découverte* (Paris, 1986), p. 217.

7. APP BA 1648, Commissaire Divisionnaire Poirson to Prefect of Police, 17 March 1937; declarations of Léon Blum in Parliamentary debate, 23 March 1937; declarations of radical Conseiller Général Georges Ory minutes of the session of the Conseil Général de la Seine, 17 March 1937, in *Bulletin Officiel de la Ville de Paris* (21 March 1937); Zevaes, *Clichy en Deuil*, pp 8–9; Moch, *Le Front Populaire, Grande Espérance*, p. 221; Jean-Paul Brunet, *Histoire du Front Populaire*, p. 82.

8. APP BA 1648, Police preparations for political meetings, 16–17 March 1937; APP BA 1648, Commissaire Divisionnaire Poirson to Prefect of Police, 17 March 1937; APP BA 1648, statement of Commissaire Divisionnaire Poirson in front of the examining magistrate Judge Beteille, 24 March 1937; declarations of the Prefect of Police, minutes of the session of the Conseil Général de la Seine, 17 March 1937, in *Bulletin Officiel de la Ville de Paris* (21 March 1937).

9. APP BA 1648, Commissaire Divisionnaire Rebut to Prefect of Police, 17 March 1937; APP BA 1648, Commissaire Divisionnaire Poirson to Prefect of Police, 17 March 1937 and 22 March 1937; APP BA 1648, Commissaire de Police, 1st arrondissement, Paris, to the Director General of the Municipal Police, 17 March 1937; APP BA 1648, Gardien de la Paix Louis Daguet to Commissaire Principal, 17 March 1937; APP BA 1648, Commissaire Principal, 6th arrondissement to Director General of Municipal Police, 17 March 1937; APP BA 1648, Gardien de la Paix Henri Van Muiswinkel to Commissaire de Police, 18 March 1937; APP BA 1648, Commissaire Principal, 4th arrondissement, Paris to Director General of Municipal Police, 18 March 1937; APP BA 1648, Commissaire Principal to Director General of Municipal Police, 19 March 1937; APP BA 1648, Brigadier Georges Houzelle to the Commissaire Principal, 19th arrondissement, Paris, 20 March 1937; APP BA 1648, statement of Commissaire Divisionnaire Poirson before Prefect of Police, 24 March 1937; APP BA 1648, statement of Commissaire Divisionnaire Poirson in front of the examining magistrate Judge Beteille, 24 March 1937; APP BA 1648, circular to all police services, signed by Marchand, Director General of the Municipal Police, 27 March 1937; Tartakowsky and Willard, *Des lendemains qui chantent?* p. 236; Zevaes, *Clichy en Deuil*, p. 10; Brunet, *Histoire du Front Populaire*, p. 82; Moch, *Le Front Populaire, Grande Espérance*, p. 222; André Cherasse, *La Hurle, La nuit sanglante de Clichy, 16 mars 1937* (Paris, 1983).

10. APP BA 1648, letter from R. Turplat, resident at Clichy, to Commissaire de Police, 16 March 1937; APP BA 1648, Commissaire, 12th arrondissement to Director General of Municipal Police, 16 March 1937; APP BA 1648, Sous-Brigadier Achille Benard to Commissaire Principal, 17 March 1937; APP BA 1648, Report from Brigadier Neige, 3rd arrondissement, 17 March 1937; APP BA 1648, report from Gardien de la Paix André Bodo to Commissaire Principal, 5th arrondissement, 17 March 1937; APP BA 1648, Commissaire Divisionnaire Poirson to Prefect of Police, 17 March 1937; APP BA 1648, Brigadier Georges Houzelle to the Commissaire Principal, 19th arrondissement, Paris, 20 March 1937; APP BA 1648, statement of Commissaire Divisionnaire Poirson in front of the examining magistrate Judge Beteille, 24 March 1937; APP BA 1648, Commissaire de Police, 15th arrondissement to Director General of Municipal Police, 25 March 1937.

11. APP BA 1648, 'Etat des agents blessés, Manifestation de Clichy', 16 March 1937; Tartakowsky & Willard, *Des lendemains qui chantent?* p. 237; Kergoat, *La*

France du Front Populaire, pp. 217–218; Moch, *Le Front Populaire, Grande Espérance*, p. 222; Borne and Dubief, *La crise des années trente*, p. 183; Seidman, *Workers against Work*, p. 296; Brunet, *Histoire du Front Populaire*, p. 82; Moch, *Le Front Populaire, Grande Espérance*, p. 222.

12. APP BA 1648, Director General of Municipal Police, Note for Prefect, 22 March 1937 and 20 April 1937; APP BA 1648, statement of Commissaire Divisionnaire Poirson in front of the examining magistrate Judge Beteille, 24 March 1937; APP BA 1648, Commissaire de Police, 15th arrondissement to Director General of Municipal Police, 25 March 1937; Paul Fleurot, minutes of the session of the Conseil Général de la Seine, 17 March 1937 in *Bulletin Officiel de la Ville de Paris* (21 March 1937); Zevaes, *Clichy en Deuil*, p. 11; Kergoat, *La France du Front Populaire, La découverte*, p. 217.

13. APP BA 1648, report from Gardien de la Paix Joseph Bourgeois to Commissaire de Police, 19th arrondissement, 19 March 1937; APP BA 1865, 'Incidents de Clichy et leurs conséquences', 19 March 1937; Socialist Conseiller Général Jean Longuet, minutes of the session of the Conseil Général de la Seine, 17 March 1937 in *Bulletin Officiel de la Ville de Paris* (21 March 1937); Zevaes, *Clichy en Deuil*, p. 10; Tartakowsky & Willard, *Des lendemains qui chantent?* pp. 236–237; Kergoat, *La France du Front Populaire, La découverte*, p. 217; Moch, *Le Front Populaire, Grande Espérance*, p. 222; Charles Serre, *Les événements survenus en France de 1933 à 1945*, Commission d'Enquête Parlementaire (Paris, 1947); Louis Ducloux, *From Blackmail to Treason: Political Crime and Corruption in France, 1920–40* (London, 1958); Jan A. Stevenson, *The Cagoule Conspiracy*; Paul Azan, *Franchet d'Espèrey* (Paris, 1949); Philippe Bourdrel, *La Cagoule: 30 ans de Complots* (Paris, 1970); Max Gallo, *Cinquième Colonne, 1930–40* (Paris, 1970); J-R Tournouz, *L'histoire secrète* (Paris, 1962); Eugen Weber, *Action Française: Royalisme and Reaction in 20th Century France* (Stanford, California, 1962); Geoffrey Warner, 'The Cagoulard Conspiracy,' *History Today* 10 (1960), pp. 443–450.

14. APP BA 1648, Brigadier Camille Fauchart to Commissaire de Police, 8th arrondissement, Paris, 26 March 1937; Archives Départementales, Bouches-du-Rhône, M6 10809 bis, Ordre du Jour du Comité du Front Populaire d'Aix-en-Provence, 23 March 1937; Jean Longuet, Georges Marrane, Vassart, Jacques Ramazotti, Frédéric Dupont, Noel Pinelli and Le Provost de Launay, minutes of the session of the Conseil Général de la Seine, 17 March 1937 in *Bulletin Officiel de la Ville de Paris* (21 March 1937); Nathaneal Greene, *Crisis and Decline: The French Socialist Party in the Popular Front Era* (Ithaca, New York, 1969), pp. 102 and 138; Tartakowsky & Willard, *Des lendemains qui chantent?* p. 237; Kergoat, *La France du Front Populaire, La découverte*, pp. 217–218; Moch, *Le Front Populaire, Grande Espérance*, p. 222; Georges Lefranc, *Histoire du Front Populaire* (Paris, 1965), p. 237; Borne & Dubief, *La crise des années trente, 1929–1938*, p. 183; Seidman, *Workers against Work*, p. 296; E. Bonnefous, *Histoire Politique de la IIIe République*, vol. 6: *Vers la guerre (1936–1938)* (Paris, 1965); Joel Colton, *Léon Blum, un socialiste à l'échelle humaine* (Paris, 1986), p. 202; Louise E. Dalby, *Léon Blum: Evolution of a Socialist* (New York, 1963), p. 312; Brunet, *Histoire du Front Populaire*, p. 82.

15. François Gabaut, 'Occultation d'un massacre: 17 octobre 1961/8 février 1962', Master's thesis, Université de Paris VII (1990); Georges Carrot, *Le maintien de l'ordre en France au XXe siècle* (Paris, 1990), p. 120; Francis Zamponi, *Les RG à l'écoute de la France* (Paris, 1997), p. 29.

3

Sectarian Violence and Police Violence in Glasgow during the 1930s

Andrew Davies

Accounts of the use of force by the police in Britain during the 1920s and 1930s have largely focused upon the policing of strikes and political meetings and demonstrations.[1] However, as Mike Brogden has shown in his oral history of policing in interwar Liverpool, everyday relations between the police and the urban working classes were characterised by a sometimes uneasy truce. Order on the streets was maintained by a combination of respect for, and fear of, the police, and new constables were taught how to wield a truncheon to disperse crowds of drunks on Saturday nights and to restore order when communal violence erupted between Protestants and Catholics.[2] In this chapter, which examines the policing of sectarian violence in Glasgow, I propose to adopt a much narrower focus. My aim is to examine the context, nature and repercussions of a single confrontation between the police and members of the Derry Boys, the junior section of a notorious Protestant street gang known as the Billy Boys, which took place on 7 August 1936.

The incident will be located in relation to the tradition of gang conflicts and street violence in Glasgow during the early twentieth century. During the 1930s, Glasgow acquired a reputation throughout Britain as a hotbed of gang violence, although the pattern of gang conflicts in the city has yet to be explored in any depth by historians.[3] Indeed, the wider history of street gangs in Britain's major cities remains largely undeveloped. Few studies have appeared since the pioneering works by Stephen Humphries and Geoffrey Pearson were published in the early 1980s.[4] Humphries and Pearson, both of whom drew their examples of 'hooliganism' from a range of British cities, located the hostility shown by gang members towards beat constables within a broader working-class resentment towards the police.[5] However, neither attempted to explore the nature or dynamics of relations between street gangs and the police in any depth. The following analysis is therefore offered both as a case-study of the policing of public order, and as an exploration of police strategies for dealing with street gangs in a specific urban milieu during the 1930s.

In Glasgow, tensions between street gangs and the police were exacerbated following the appointment of Percy Sillitoe as the city's Chief Constable in November 1931. Sillitoe, labelled 'Britain's Ace Gang Buster' by an admiring popular press, moved to Glasgow from Sheffield where he had been widely acclaimed following a campaign to suppress the vendettas between rival gangs wrestling for control of the city's illegal gaming pitches.[6] In Glasgow, Sillitoe again devoted considerable police resources to a campaign against local 'gangsters'.[7] However, despite a series of high profile trials, Glasgow's street gangs posed recurring difficulties for Sillitoe, and by the summer of 1936 he faced increasing pressure to deal with a reported escalation of gang violence in the city's East End.

The nature of the confrontation between the police and the Derry Boys in August 1936 is investigated here through an analysis of press reports and court records relating to the ensuing court cases.[8] These contemporary accounts are examined alongside Sillitoe's own version of events, published almost twenty years later, in his autobiography, *Cloak without Dagger*.[9] Sillitoe's retrospective account, which provides a clear statement of the utility of police violence, presents a rare opportunity to re-examine the versions of events given by police officers in the immediate aftermath of a confrontation between the police and a hostile crowd. The repercussions of the confrontation between the police and the Derry Boys are initially explored through an assessment of the response of the Glasgow magistrates to the police action. The impact of the confrontation and subsequent trial upon the pattern of gang conflicts in the city is then assessed in order to evaluate Sillitoe's assertion that he had effectively curbed the notorious Glasgow gangs by the mid-1930s.[10]

Street Gangs in Glasgow in the 1920s and 1930s

Gang conflicts were an enduring feature of life in Glasgow's work-ing-class districts throughout the late-nineteenth and early-twenti-eth centuries.[11] The city's street gangs tended to be organised primarily (although not exclusively) as fighting gangs.[12] Gang members strove to enhance their status and reputation, both col-lectively and as individuals, by taking part in street fighting and considerable peer-group prestige was at stake in clashes between rival gangs. Young people tended to join gangs in their mid-teens, and a survey of the city's gangs published by the *Evening Citizen* in 1930 claimed that the majority of gang members were aged between seventeen and twenty-one.[13] However, as the scale of long-term unemployment grew in Glasgow during the 1930s, it became increasingly common for those aged in their twenties and even early thirties to play leading roles in the gangs.[14] The major-ity of gang members were male, but as the local press was quick to point out, young women also occasionally took an active part in street fighting and some of the most prominent gangs were reputed to have 'Queens' who were renowned for their fighting prowess.[15]

Rival gangs confronted each other in streets, dance halls and cinemas across the working-class districts of the city, frequently in response to incursions by members of one gang into the territory of another. In contrast to their counterparts in the United States, Glas-gow's 'gangsters' eschewed firearms and fought instead with bro-ken bottles, knives, bayonets, clubs and, on occasion, razors.[16] Accounts of disturbances given in Glasgow's courtrooms (and widely reported in the local press) suggest that gang fighting was to some extent ritualised, and whilst weapons were widely used, fatalities were rare.[17] Nonetheless, as retrospective accounts by for-mer gang members testify, severe woundings were commonplace and many 'gangsters' bore scars as lasting reminders of their youthful pursuit of status and reprisal.[18] Not surprisingly, gang conflicts posed considerable operational difficulties for the city's police force during the interwar decades, with isolated beat con-stables in particular risking severe injury in their efforts to break up fights between gangs armed with bottles, razors and clubs.[19]

By the mid-1930s, civic leaders were increasingly alarmed by the negative depictions of Glasgow's gang conflicts in the English press, fearing that the city's trading prospects, already blighted by the label 'Red Clydeside', were being further damaged by articles comparing Glasgow's 'gangsters' with those of Chicago.[20] It must be stressed that Glasgow's gang conflicts were tame affairs by comparison with those witnessed in the United States during the Prohibition era.[21] The lower level of violence in Glasgow can be explained in large part by the much lower economic stakes in the city's gang conflicts. Street gangs did operate protection rackets in Glasgow's working-class districts during the 1920s and 1930s, and publicans, small shopkeepers, market traders, illicit bookmakers and the proprietors and managers of cinemas and dance halls were all allegedly targeted.[22] Moreover, one of the city's gangs (the Beehive Boys from the Gorbals in Glasgow's South Side) acquired a reputation as a team of criminal specialists which included housebreakers, 'smash and grab' raiders, fraudsters and a safe-blower.[23] However, when compared to the vast fortunes attributed to the leading figures in the Chicago underworld during Prohibition, the profits enjoyed by Glasgow's 'gangsters' were paltry.[24]

Glasgow's gang conflicts were most intense in the working-class districts of the South Side and East End. For the most part, South Side gangs tended to be primarily territorial in their affiliations. By contrast, those drawn from the East End of the city tended to be both territorial and sectarian, and the most powerful gangs in the East End districts of the Calton and Bridgeton were overtly Protestant or Catholic formations.[25] Sectarian violence was a manifestation of the long-standing antipathy between Glasgow's Protestant majority and the city's Catholic population, the majority of whom were of Irish descent.[26] In the East End, sectarian tensions were exacerbated by the influence of the Protestant Irish who had settled in the Calton and Bridgeton districts during the nineteenth century, bringing with them the sectarian culture and politics of Ulster.[27]

Most notably, Bridgeton formed one of the Glasgow strongholds of the Orange Order, the bastion of militant Protestantism whose Twelfth of July parades commemorated the victory of the Protestant William of Orange – 'King Billy' – at the Battle of the Boyne in Ireland in 1690.[28] The annual 'Orange Walks' were usually held in a town or village outside Glasgow, and reportedly drew as many as 100,000 participants and supporters from the West of Scotland (including large contingents from Glasgow) and Northern Ireland during the interwar decades. The walks were held on Saturdays, and the return of the Glasgow processionists invariably led to widespread outbreaks of street violence across the city, with the worst incidents generally reported in the East End.[29] Protestant gang members attached themselves to the processions in order to protect the participants as they ventured homeward through the city. However, the presence of recognised gangs of street fighters served only to heighten the sense of provocation as the returning processionists entered thoroughfares routinely occupied by Catholic street gangs. The violent clashes which frequently ensued appear to have been relished by Protestant and Catholic gangs alike.[30] Large-scale outbreaks of sectarian street fighting were by no means confined to the Twelfth of July parades. Smaller Protestant church parades frequently led to skirmishes involving several hundred people, and Catholic processions, whether organised by the churches or by the Ancient Order of Hibernians, were likewise marred by communal violence.[31]

Gang members also featured prominently in the collective violence which surrounded sporting events in Glasgow. Throughout the interwar decades, rival followers of the Rangers and Celtic football clubs (identified respectively as emblems of Protestantism and Catholicism) clashed before, during and after matches between the two teams. Moreover, Celtic supporters risked ambush whenever they travelled to their team's stadium which was situated close to the East End Protestant stronghold of Bridgeton Cross.[32] Matches between Rangers and Celtic, like the city's religious parades, effectively served to mobilise bigotry amongst the adherents of both faiths, with members of rival territorial gangs temporarily joining forces to enact over-arching sectarian hostilities.[33]

The Bridgeton Billy Boys

During the late 1920s and 1930s, the Billy Boys of Bridgeton Cross were widely recognised as the most powerful of Glasgow's gangs.[34] The gang was founded by Billy Fullerton in 1924 following a fray on Glasgow Green between a group of Protestant youths from Bridgeton and Catholic youths who belonged to the Kent Star gang from the Calton. Fullerton, who was then aged eighteen, subsequently claimed to have been struck with a hammer during the fray. His associates decided to form a gang of their own in order to seek revenge, and Fullerton became leader of a thirty-strong group on the grounds that he was considered to be the strongest fighter amongst them.[35] By naming themselves the Billy Boys, and thus invoking the victory of King Billy at the Battle of the Boyne, Fullerton and his associates ensured that the gang would serve as a constant vehicle for sectarian violence. Claiming Bridgeton Cross as their territory, the Billy Boys became an immediate focus for Protestant youths in the locality and they were soon notorious for their involvement in clashes with Catholic street gangs from the surrounding area.[36]

By 1927, the ranks of the Billy Boys had swollen to an estimated 200 for the occasion of the annual Twelfth of July parade.[37] At their peak during the 1930s, they boasted 800 members, mostly drawn from Bridgeton but with additional support from nearby Lanarkshire towns such as Airdrie and Coatbridge. Uniquely amongst Glasgow's street gangs, the Billy Boys developed elements of paramilitary organisation. The gang's members were divided into thirty- or forty-strong sections with recognised section commanders and a system of fines and court martials.[38] During the 1930s, the Billy Boys also established a 'junior section', known as the Derry Boys, comprised of 'lads' aged between fourteen and twenty-one. The Derry Boys provided apprenticeships in street fighting and formed both a powerful gang in their own right and an effective recruiting ground for the senior Billy Boys.[39]

The Billy Boys amassed substantial funds to support the gang's activities. Members paid dues of two pence per week, with further monies raised through lotteries and dances held in Glasgow and in towns across Lanarkshire.[40] According to the local press, they also operated protection rackets throughout the East End. Small shopkeepers, publicans and café owners were particular targets, with 'Bridgeton and Calton ... divided into areas for the purpose of systematic collection.'[41] At the height of the gang's organisation, the Billy Boys held £1,200 in a Bridgeton bank. This was a considerable sum in a period when the average weekly wage of a manual worker stood at around three pounds, even if Billy Fullerton, clearly, was no Al Capone.[42] Funds were used to pay fines on behalf of the gang's members, and to support the families of those in prison.[43]

The Billy Boys issued membership cards which bore the pledge 'To uphold King, Country and Constitution ... [and] to defend other Protestants'.[44] To an extent which was again unique amongst the city's street gangs, the Billy Boys made a series of interventions in local politics. On at least one occasion, the gang provided stewards for a Unionist campaign meeting in the East End prior to the 1931 general election.[45] At local elections, the Billy Boys switched their allegiance to the more militant Scottish Protestant League, whose meetings at times degenerated into free fights between the Billy Boys and members of Catholic gangs such as the Norman Conks.[46] Under the leadership of Fullerton, an active Fascist, the Billy Boys also disrupted Communist Party meetings and demonstrations and attacked marches organised by the Communist-inspired National Unemployed Workers' Movement.[47] Not surprisingly, the Billy Boys played a very prominent part in the outbreaks of communal violence which marred both religious processions throughout Glasgow and matches involving the Rangers football club.[48] However, most of the reported outbreaks of street violence involving the Billy Boys and the Derry Boys consisted of territorial skirmishes with Catholic street gangs in the East End such as the Norman Conks, the Calton Entry, the Kent Star, the Cheeky Forty, the Savoy Arcadians and the Shanley Boys.

Sillitoe and the Gangs

In Percy Sillitoe's own view, his appointment as Chief Constable of Glasgow in November 1931 was largely due to his success in dealing with the 'gangsters' of Sheffield.[49] Glasgow's gang conflicts had been the subject of enormous local anxiety throughout the summer of 1930 when a series of highly-publicised cases prompted considerable local speculation concerning both the causes of gang violence and strategies for dealing with the problem.[50] Sillitoe, who cherished his reputation as a 'gang buster', inevitably placed local street gangs high on his agenda from the moment of his appointment.

Most of the outbreaks of gang violence which were brought to Sillitoe's attention following his arrival in Glasgow were clustered either in Bridgeton in the East End or in the Gorbals district in the city's South Side. Some of the most serious disturbances in the East End involved clashes between the Billy Boys and the Norman Conks, who regularly raided each other's territory, leading to frays in which knives, bottles, pickshafts, hatchets and other weapons were used.[51] To the consternation of the police, the Billy Boys formed a flute and drum band which regularly marched into Catholic neighbourhoods such as Norman Street playing well-known 'Orange' tunes. Full-scale gang fights frequently ensued. As Sillitoe pointed out, these were difficult incidents to police since officers arriving at the scene were bombarded with missiles from both sides.[52] Sillitoe described Billy Fullerton, the leader of the Billy Boys, as an ingenious, if reckless, general who 'derived considerable pleasure and excitement from pitting his gangsters against the Norman Conks.'[53]

Sillitoe's strategy for dealing with the city's street gangs was carefully coordinated. Upon his arrival in Glasgow, he compiled a historical profile of gang activity in the city, interviewing long-serving police officers and studying police incident files to assess the composition and organisation of the gangs.[54] Maps of each police division were then posted at police headquarters, and the dates, times and locations of all reported incidents were marked on the maps with coloured flags in order to study the pattern of gang activity in the city.[55] As part of a general scheme to overhaul Glasgow's police communications systems, police boxes were erected across the city with telephone links to divisional headquarters to enable more rapid responses.[56] Under Sillitoe, the Glasgow force also invested heavily in motor technology, increasing the use of patrol vans and cars, some of which were equipped with radios, so that 'flying squads' could be mobilised to deal with incidents across the city.[57] Sillitoe recruited networks of paid informers, including bar staff employed in public houses, and a squad of 'special irregulars' (including ex-boxers) to be sent out in vans with regular police officers to 'fight the gangs'.[58] According to Sillitoe's biographer, A.W. Cockerill, 'Sillitoe was known to have had some gangsters committed for observation to a mental institution where they were confined for a period beyond their sentence. They were then released on the threat of being permanently certified should they for any reason be returned to jail.' This highly-illegal tactic must have formed a much more potent threat than imprisonment, and Cockerill claimed the threat caused some 'gangsters' to leave Glasgow permanently.[59] Finally, Sillitoe threatened to ban matches between the Rangers and Celtic football clubs, although he received an anonymous death threat in return and the ban was never imposed.[60]

Early in 1934, two years into his period of office in Glasgow, Sillitoe issued a warning to the city's gangs in an interview published by a popular Sunday newspaper. Sillitoe declared that the police were determined to fight the city's 'gangsters' with the 'utmost ferocity' in order to 'teach them that they must take heed of the law'.[61] In February 1934, ten members of the Beehive Boys gang from the Gorbals stood trial at Glasgow Sheriff Court on charges relating to a series of property crimes, frays at South Side dance halls, and assaults upon police officers. The Beehive Boys were targeted because they were perceived to be the gang most heavily involved in systematic offences against property. Eight of the gang's members were convicted and their leader, Peter Williamson, was gaoled for twelve months.[62] The trial attracted extensive publicity in the local press, as Sillitoe no doubt intended. However, if the trial of the Beehive Boys was intended as a warning to the city's 'gangsters', it appears to have had little effect other than to spur the gangs on to ever more fearsome displays of violence. Within a fortnight, James Dalziel, the leader of another Gorbals-based gang, was fatally stabbed by an East End 'gangster' in an affray at the Bedford Parlour dance hall, and the Billy Boys launched a violent and highly-publicised ambush on a train full of Celtic football supporters.[63]

Gang conflicts continued to capture headlines in the local and national press over the course of the next twelve months.[64] In July 1935, the notoriety of the Billy Boys was further heightened when their flute band travelled to Belfast for the annual Orange Walk.[65] The summer of 1935 saw sectarian disturbances in Belfast which eclipsed anything seen in Glasgow during the 1930s.[66] Ten people (seven Protestants and three Catholics) were killed in the rioting in Belfast and more than eighty people severely injured, many with gunshot wounds.[67] A large number of Catholic families were driven out of their homes in predominantly Protestant districts.[68] The most serious riot followed a march by 3,000–4,000 people to deliver a wreath to the home of a Protestant youth who had been shot dead the previous evening. The marchers proceeded to the Catholic lower dock area of the city, shouting 'redd [clear] them out'. As A.C. Hepburn has noted, the marchers were headed by the Billy Boys' band.[69] Of course, we cannot attribute the outbreaks of sectarian rioting in Belfast to the presence of the Billy Boys. Nonetheless, the Glasgow 'gangsters' appear to have helped to inflame the situation. Marching their band into predominantly Catholic neighbourhoods was the gang's forte, and the Billy Boys showed a clear willingness to take a leading part in the troubles in Belfast.

In October 1935, press coverage of the 'gangsters' reign of terror' in Glasgow was greatly intensified following the publication of the novel *No Mean City*. Co-authored by Alexander McArthur, an unemployed Glasgow baker, *No Mean City* told the story of a local gang leader and 'razor king', and featured a series of graphic accounts of gang violence.[70] *No Mean City* attracted enormous attention in the Scottish, English and international press, cementing Glasgow's reputation as a violent city to the dismay of local civic leaders and industrialists.[71] This heightened concern with the city's 'gang menace' formed the backdrop to the events of August 1936.

7 August 1936

The confrontation between the police and the Derry Boys (the junior section of the Bridgeton Billy Boys) on 7 August 1936 followed the escalation of gang conflicts in the East End of Glasgow during the month following the annual Orange walk. The confrontation and its repercussions are worth examining in some depth in order both to document the use of force by the police and to assess the responses to police violence amongst civic leaders and the local press as well as amongst the working-class population of the East End.

On Saturday 11 July 1936, a crowd estimated at more than 100,000 (including fifty-eight bands) travelled from across the west of Scotland and Belfast to Airdrie in Lanarkshire for the parade to commemorate the Battle of the Boyne. As the Glasgow processionists returned later that night, disturbances broke out across the city. The worst outbreaks occurred in the North Side where a police officer was taken to hospital following 'running fights' in which bottles and stones were thrown, but twenty people were also arrested during disturbances in the East End.[72] Sporadic sectarian disturbances continued in the East End during the second half of July. In one incident in Nuneaton Street in Bridgeton, two men reportedly fought a duel with bayonets in front of a crowd of 300 people.[73]

In late July, the Derry Boys were enraged when members of a rival gang 'interfered with' a funeral at Sandymount Cemetery.[74] This sparked an intensification of sectarian street fighting in Bridgeton, with a spate of disturbances involving rival gangs reported during the first week of August. A local resident wrote to John Stewart, Lord Provost of Glasgow, complaining that 'the trouble was being aggravated by inflammatory speeches of a so-called religious description' and asking for steps to be taken to deal with the problem. The Lord Provost forwarded the letter to Percy Sillitoe, who replied that he had drafted extra officers into Bridgeton and added that the police were 'generally taking greater precautions there'.[75] On Wednesday 5 August, the Derry Boys paraded through Bridgeton with the Billy Boys' flute band, provoking a series of confrontations with Catholic street gangs.[76] On Friday 7 August, the Derry Boys again started to parade with the band, setting off from Bridgeton Cross at 7.40 p.m.

According to initial press reports, events unfolded as follows: the band's followers were highly disorderly, throwing bottles, sticks and stones, and in London Road, members of the procession attacked the police. Contingency plans had been made to deal with any trouble that occurred, and mounted police and patrol vans full of additional officers were rushed to the scene. The police were forced to charge the procession with their batons drawn. Twenty-five arrests were made, and 'minor' injuries were sustained by some of those arrested in the melee.[77] This version of events, which was subsequently to be challenged at the Glasgow Sheriff's Court, appears to have been supplied to the local press by the police.

The police maintained a heavy presence in Bridgeton into the early hours of the morning, but members of local gangs (who had likewise expected trouble that night) also took to the streets.[78] At around 9.00 p.m., an off-duty Detective Constable was assaulted and badly beaten in Shettleston Road.[79] At 11.00 p.m., the police dispersed a crowd of around 300 people gathered at Bridgeton Cross. The crowd retaliated by damaging property, smashing the plate-glass window of a shop nearby.[80] At midnight, with gangs still gathered on street corners, the police patrolled the district in vans.[81] Bottles were thrown at press reporters' cars as they drove around the area.[82]

In the aftermath of the confrontation between the police and the Derry Boys, Glasgow's police and magistrates closed ranks in a concerted attempt to curb gang conflicts in the city's East End. Twenty-four of those arrested during the melee between the police and the Derry Boys appeared at the Eastern Police Court the following morning (Saturday 8 August), where they were charged with forming part of a disorderly crowd and committing a breach of the peace. They were remanded in custody by Bailie Matthew Armstrong. Six of the accused appeared in court with their heads bandaged.[83] The police maintained a heavy presence in Bridgeton throughout the day on Saturday, anticipating further outbreaks of violence. Nonetheless, a series of disturbances took place at Bridgeton Cross, with members of the Derry Boys reportedly taking part in at least four of these incidents. The gang's alleged leader, 'Killer' McKay, was arrested following a fight which involved around thirty men at Bridgeton Cross at 10.20 p.m.[84]

On Sunday 9 August, the Glasgow-based *Sunday Mail* published an article by Bailie Armstrong, in which he denounced the gangsters of the East End as 'religious illiterates' and 'pests of the vilest order'. Declaring that 'We cannot allow the good name of our city to be dragged in the mud by bands of hooligans,' Armstrong called for 'gangsters' to face gaol sentences (since fines would be levied from local shopkeepers) and for police patrols to be trebled in districts where gang fighting was most prevalent. Armstrong concluded with a plea for religious tolerance, imploring 'Let us be done all at once and once for all with this degrading conduct.'[85] His plea was ignored. That afternoon saw a series of parades around Bridgeton by sectarian bands and their followers. The processions were closely monitored by the police but were nevertheless punctuated by minor outbreaks of disorder. In Baltic Street, rival gangs fought with sticks, batons and iron bars, whilst in Arcadia Street, a police constable escorting a band was struck by a bottle thrown from a tenement window.[86]

On Monday 10 August, seventeen people (including nine Derry Boys) were sentenced at the Eastern Police Court to terms of between fourteen and sixty days' imprisonment following breaches of the peace in Bridgeton on Saturday and Sunday.[87] The police continued to station extra officers in the district, including mounted constables, and patrol cars were diverted to Bridgeton from across Glasgow to increase the mobility of reinforcements.[88] On 11 August, the Glasgow magistrates, prompted by the Lord Provost, appointed a special subcommittee to deal with the problems posed by the city's street gangs and requested a report on the issue from the Chief Constable.[89] Alert to claims that the gangs routinely raised payments for fines from terrified local shopkeepers, the Lord Provost told the *Evening Citizen* that the magistrates should 'stop fining these people' and start imposing prison sentences for gang members as matter of course.[90] An anonymous magistrate interviewed by the *Evening Times* showed strong support for Sillitoe, declaring that 'The police are handling the situation with great courage and considerable tact … but their efforts must be backed up by all the resources of the law.' In the magistrate's view, 'a touch of the lash' was the only way to deal with 'extreme cases'.[91] Renewed outbreaks of sectarian street fighting over the course of the week duly led to the imposition of exemplary sentences of sixty days' imprisonment at the Eastern Police Court.[92]

Saturday 15 August saw further outbreaks of gang violence. Members of the Derry Boys caused a fray in an Ancient Order of Hibernians dance hall in Greenvale Street. Two men were arrested at the scene, one of whom allegedly struck a police constable with a broken glass. In a separate incident, a police constable was threatened by members of the Norman Conks, five of whom were arrested after a police patrol van was summoned to the scene. Prison sentences were imposed upon the accused in both cases at the Eastern Police Court on 17 August.[93] On the same day, the twenty-four people arrested during the confrontation between the police and the Derry Boys on 7 August appeared at the Glasgow Sheriff Court, where the date for their trial was set for 14 September. The prisoners all pleaded not guilty, and bail was set at ten pounds per head by Sheriff Robertson.[94] Within two days, 'four persons who wish to remain anonymous' had paid the combined bail costs of £240.[95] This must testify either to the solid financial organisation of the Billy Boys' (or perhaps to their prowess as 'racketeers') or to the tacit support of more affluent sections of Glasgow's Protestant community, some of whom were not averse to hiring the Billy Boys to break up left-wing political meetings.[96]

The magistrates' subcommittee dealing with the 'gangster menace' met Percy Sillitoe on 21 August. At the end of the meeting, the magistrates announced their collective intention to mete out 'severe and exemplary terms of imprisonment, without the option of a fine' for those convicted of charges involving the 'gang and hooligan element'.[97] The police claimed that the situation in Bridgeton was much quieter over the weekend of 22–23 August despite several religious processions taking place, leading the local press to ponder whether 'this strange peace' reflected the continued deployment of extra police in Bridgeton or the recent statement by the magistrates.[98] On 31 August, the magistrates issued a formal resolution stating their intention to gaol all those charged with gang-related offences or the use of lethal weapons. The magistrates further appealed to the press not to give 'undue publicity' to such cases, particularly by publishing the names and addresses of those convicted.[99]

When the trial of the twenty-three men and one woman arrested during the Derry Boys' parade on 7 August commenced at the Glasgow Sheriff Court on 14 September, they faced charges of disorderly conduct and committing a breach of the peace.[100] The police evidence was presented by Lieutenant James White, who told how at 7.40 p.m. on the evening of 7 August, the police received a message that a flute band was proceeding East along London Road with a crowd of disorderly followers. Forty police officers in three patrol vans drove past the band, which was accompanied by a crowd of around 500 people who were shouting sectarian slogans and waving orange and blue (Rangers Football Club) colours. The police vans drew up in front of the band, and Lieutenant White asked where they were going. When he received no reply, he told them that they were to proceed no further. The crowd then became menacing. A member of the crowd made a thrust at a police officer with a spear, and stones were thrown at the police. White ordered his officers to draw their batons and apprehend the members of the crowd.[101]

Several other officers gave similar evidence in support of White's account, insisting that police only drew their batons after the band leader had issued the instruction to march on, and stones had been thrown at the police.[102] A number of weapons, including spears, wooden batons, iron bars and pieces of lead, were displayed on a wall in the courtroom. According to the police, all of these weapons had been brandished by members of crowd on 7 August.[103]

The defence witnesses included four women who made allegations of police brutality. According to their testimonies, the band had stopped playing and their leader was turning them around when the police made an unprovoked baton charge. The women claimed that they had witnessed the melee as passers-by, but had themselves been assaulted by the police. Mrs Mary Rennie told how the disorder had been caused by the police: 'They were hitting everybody, and people were shouting from their windows "The poor bandsmen, the poor bandsmen."' A Mrs Watson alleged that how she had been holding a child in her arms when a police officer struck at her with a baton. Sixty-year-old Mrs Margaret Usher claimed that she was standing at the corner of the street when the police made their baton charge. Two police officers grabbed her and pinned her arms behind her back. She was put into a police van and told to lie on the floor. At the police station, she protested that she had nothing to do with the band, and was told to 'get out'. Asked whether it had been a very brutal attack, she replied: 'It wasn't half. I have never seen such a brutal attack in my life. It was worse than the General Strike.'[104]

Nineteen of the twenty-three male prisoners were convicted, with the charges against the remaining four 'not proven'. Sheriff Kermack described the case as arising from a 'deliberate challenge' to the forces of law and order, and insisted that he had no option but to impose sentences of imprisonment upon those found guilty. He gaoled each of them for one month. The lone female prisoner, Isabella Scott, was also convicted, but her sentence of fourteen days' imprisonment was deferred for six months, with Kermack commenting that: 'in view of her sex and age he was unwilling to send her to prison. He considered her a foolish girl who had somehow or other got mixed up in the disturbance.'[105]

Kermack appeared to be untroubled when faced with two conflicting accounts of the incident. He declared firmly that the discrepancies in the police testimonies were only such as 'one expected to find from honest witnesses in such circumstances'. However, he declared that he was unimpressed by the quality of the evidence for defence: 'It was not independent in his view, and did not impress him as being genuine evidence, but rather as having been given with some ulterior motive.' Turning to the allegation that the police had used unnecessary violence in dealing with the 'riot', Kermack proclaimed that: 'The use of force by the police is a necessary matter, and when used has to be used in a determined manner. How far it is to be used must be, to a large extent, left to the discretion of the officers in charge at the time.'[106] Of course, the discrepancies in accounts of police and defence witnesses are hardly surprising. No doubt there were elements of truth in both sets of accounts, but it is difficult to gauge the quality of the competing testimonies, not least since there are no full transcripts of the evidence presented at the trial. The edited highlights reported by the local press effectively constitute the only surviving record of the courtroom exchanges.

Sillitoe's autobiography, however, casts further light on the events of 7 August. Almost two decades later, Sillitoe told how he backed Lieutenant White's decision to use force to suppress the parades by the Billy Boys' band.[107] White then organised an ambush of the band and its followers in London Road. According to Sillitoe's retrospective account, the police fully expected the band to try to sweep past the police officers who blocked their path. When they did so, mounted police who had been strategically positioned in a side street immediately charged the band and its followers who were then easily apprehended by squads of officers on foot. In Sillitoe's account, the police used 'long riot batons' to scatter the parade, leaving the road 'littered with casualties' as they made their arrests. Only one of the band's members escaped injury in the melee. According to Sillitoe, this 'wholesale defeat' was the 'beginning of the end for the Billy Boys'.[108] Sillitoe recalled that there had been a 'tremendous outcry' against police brutality, but appears to have taken some pleasure in the label 'Sillitoe's Cossacks' which the press attached to the mounted police. Sillitoe declared, 'I was proud to stand by Inspector White in what he did.'[109]

Sillitoe's version of events appears to lend powerful retrospective support to the statements by defence witnesses at the trial. Sillitoe was keen to stress his officers' capacity to beat the 'gangsters' at their own game, and he appears to have basked in the reputed toughness of his men, just as Billy Fullerton did as leader of the Billy Boys. Nonetheless, Sillitoe's admission in 1955 that the police had planned to rout the Billy Boys, and had deployed mounted officers and issued long riot batons accordingly, suggests that the police recognised in 1936 that force was their only effective means to combat the most powerful of Glasgow's street gangs. The local establishment was only too willing to back both Sillitoe's judgement and his methods. Speaking at a dinner for local civic and business leaders which coincided with the conclusion of the trial at

Glasgow Sheriff Court on 22 September, Sheriff Samuel McDonald proclaimed that:

> he could say with the utmost confidence and after considerable thought, that the gang menace in Glasgow was not a menace at all.
>
> He knew for a fact ... that the police in the city had got the matter of the gangs well in hand, and would, in the course of a short time, have it effectively dealt with.[110]

Sillitoe as a 'Gang Buster'

To what extent did the ambush of the Derry Boys and the Billy Boys' flute band on 7 August constitute a decisive victory in Sillitoe's campaign to curb the Glasgow gangs? The rout of the Billy Boys' 'junior section' led to heightened tensions in the East End which in turn met with saturation policing and the imposition of harsh sentences by the city's magistrates. By late August and September, the local press reported only sporadic clashes between rival gangs in Bridgeton, and there were no further confrontations between gang members and the police on the scale witnessed on 7 August. In the short-term, the police action thus appears to have defused a spate of bitter sectarian gang-fighting.[111]

In assessing the longer-term impact of this show of strength by the police, however, we must be more cautious. Sillitoe's own account of how he curbed the Glasgow gangs hinged upon his retrospective reordering of a sequence of events which, when viewed in their proper chronological sequence, suggest that the ambush of 7 August 1936 formed part of a more complex and enduring struggle between the gangs and the police.[112] Whereas Sillitoe claimed that he had effectively suppressed gang warfare in Glasgow by the mid-1930s, reports in the local press reveal that street gangs continued to pose severe problems for the Glasgow police until the eve of Second World War.[113] Viewed from this perspective, the police ambush of the Derry Boys marked little more than a temporary lull in the broader pattern of conflicts between rival gangs, and the ongoing tensions between the city's 'gangsters' and the police. Within a month of the trial of the Derry Boys in September 1936, a member of a Catholic street gang in Bridgeton died from knife wounds following a fight with members of his own gang, who had accused him of fraternising with the Billy Boys. The subsequent trial at the Glasgow High Court exposed the simmering sectarian hostilities which continued to plague the city's East End and prompted a renewed doubling of police patrols in known trouble spots in Bridgeton.[114]

Under Sillitoe, the Glasgow police succeeded only in containing the city's gang conflicts. Squads of officers arriving in patrol vans usually broke up clashes between rival gangs very quickly. However, the police were unable to prevent gang violence from erupting. Gang conflicts were too firmly embedded in the culture of Glasgow's working-class districts, and ranged over such wide areas of the city that the police were unable to mount constant surveillance of all of the potential trouble spots. Police officers in Glasgow were frequently bombarded with missiles by hostile crowds, but the city's 'gangsters' appear to have respected the 'polis' for their toughness and few were willing to fight either beat constables or detectives at close quarters unless the police were greatly outnumbered.[115] Police officers, like the self-styled 'gangsters' themselves, appear to have cultivated reputations as 'hard' men, and we might accept Seán Damer's depiction of the police as, in effect, the most powerful 'gang' in the city.[116] Nonetheless, the maintenance of order in the working-class districts colonised by the gangs posed ongoing problems for the police.

The resort to force by the police in August 1936 was clearly driven by political pressure. Concerned at the potential political and economic costs of Glasgow's growing reputation as a city in the thrall of 'gangsterdom', the Lord Provost demanded firm action on the part of the city's police. Percy Sillitoe, who basked in the reputed toughness of the men under his command in both Sheffield and Glasgow, was happy to oblige. The city's magistrates and sheriffs, heavily prompted by the Lord Provost and by the local press, closed ranks behind the police. A rash of prison sentences was accompanied by fierce denouncements of the city's gangsters, and complaints of police brutality were brusquely dismissed. The local press, which shared the Lord Provost's concern at the industrial and commercial costs of Glasgow's reputation for 'gangsterdom', duly applauded the implementation of more severe sentences and found little reason to question police tactics.[117] It was left to Sillitoe, eager, after nearly twenty years, to claim credit for cleaning the city of 'evil', to reveal the extent to which the police were willing to deploy force in a pre-emptive strike against the most powerful of the Glasgow's street gangs. Sillitoe's retrospective acknowledgement that he viewed violence as a necessary and legitimate police tactic provides a useful corrective to views of

the 1930s as a 'golden age' of urban policing in Britain, in which
beat constables formed part of the fabric of the 'community'. In
Glasgow, as in London, Liverpool and elsewhere in urban Britain,
police officers were well aware of the utility of the truncheon and
residents of the poorer working-class districts knew only too well
that the potency of the police ultimately rested upon their monopoly of legitimate force.[118]

Notes

1. Clive Emsley, *The English Police: A Political and Social History*, 2nd ed., (London, 1996), pp. 137–143.
2. Mike Brogden, *On the Mersey Beat: Policing Liverpool between the Wars* (Oxford, 1991), pp. 102–10. See also Jerry White, *The Worst Street in North London: Campbell Bunk, Islington, between the Wars* (London, 1986), pp. 114–21.
3. For Glasgow's reputation as a city terrorised by violent gangs, see the *Sunday Dispatch*, 10 March 1935; *Sunday Mail*, 16 June 1935; and the *Glasgow Herald*, 24 December 1936. Bill Murray's *The Old Firm: Sectarianism, Sport and Society in Scotland* (Edinburgh, 1984) provides one of the few effective academic treatments of the subject.
4. Stephen Humphries, *Hooligans or Rebels? An Oral History of Working-Class Childhood and Youth 1889–1939* (Oxford, 1981); Geoffrey Pearson, *Hooligan: A History of Respectable Fears* (London, 1983).
5. Humphries, *Hooligans or Rebels*, pp. 203–6; Pearson, *Hooligan*, pp. 85–9.
6. J. P. Bean (pseud.), *The Sheffield Gang Wars* (Sheffield, 1981), pp. 121–9.
7. Sir Percy Sillitoe, *Cloak without Dagger* (London, 1955), pp. 122–35, A.W. Cockerill, *Sir Percy Sillitoe* (London, 1975), pp. 132–3, 140–8. Sillitoe's own memoir presents a dramatic account of his activities as a 'gang buster'. However, he reordered key events to present his period of office in Glasgow in a more flattering light. For example, the murder of James Dalziel in a gang fight in a South Side dance hall, described by Sillitoe as having taken place in 1924, in fact occurred in 1934. Compare Sillitoe, *Cloak without Dagger*, pp. 126–7, with the *Sunday Mail*, 4 March 1934.
8. The Glasgow press, including the *Glasgow Herald, Daily Record, Evening Citizen, Evening Times, Sunday Mail* and *Sunday Post*, provided extensive coverage of the incident and subsequent trial between 8 August and 23 September 1936. A record of the trial at the Glasgow Sheriff Court is held at the Scottish Record Office, SC36/57/19, case no. 5553.
9. Sillitoe, *Cloak without Dagger*, pp. 130–31.
10. Sillitoe, *Cloak without Dagger*, pp. 133–5.
11. Murray, *Old Firm*, pp. 147–9, James Patrick (pseud.), *A Glasgow Gang Observed* (London, 1973), pp. 149–52.
12. See the 'Truth about Glasgow Gangs', *Evening Citizen*, 4, 6, 7, 8 August 1930.
13. *Evening Citizen*, 6 August 1930.
14. Significantly, gangs with older memberships, such as the Beehive Boys of the Gorbals district and the Bridgeton Billy Boys, were viewed by the police as posing the most serious threat to property and public order during the 1930s.

See Andrew Davies, 'Street Gangs, Crime and Policing in Glasgow during the 1930s: The case of the Beehive Boys', *Social History* 23, 3 (1998), p. 258.

15. For reports of female involvement in gang fighting, see the *Weekly Record*, 1 June 1929; *Evening Citizen*, 7 August 1930.

16. *Sunday Dispatch*, 10 March 1935; Sillitoe, *Cloak without Dagger*, pp. 125–6.

17. Davies, *Street Gangs and Violence*.

18. For retrospective accounts by former gang members, see the *Weekly Record*, 28 June 1930 and the *Evening Citizen*, 17, 18, 19, 21 January 1955. On the prevalence of facial scars among gang members, see Davies, 'Street Gangs, Crime and Policing', p. 258. For a contrasting assessment of the level of violence in gang conflicts in British cities in the late nineteenth and early twentieth centuries, see Humphries, *Hooligans or Rebels*, pp. 190–93.

19. Robert Colquhoun, *Life Begins at Midnight* (London, 1962), pp. 18, 35–6.

20. For the currency of Glasgow's label as the 'Scotch Chicago', see *The Sunday Mail*, 16 June 1935. For an account of Glasgow's image as 'Red Clydeside' (on account of the militancy of the local labour movement during and after the First World War), see Seán Damer, *Glasgow: Going for a Song* (London, 1990), pp. 116–36.

21. Chicago saw 136 gang-related murders during the first five years of Prohibition according to Edward Behr, *Prohibition: Thirteen Years that Changed America* (New York, 1996), p. 186.

22. Reports of 'racketeering' by 'gangsters' were very frequently carried by the local press. See for example the *Weekly Record*, 20 December 1930; *Glasgow Weekly Herald*, 18 June 1932; *Sunday Mail*, 10 July 1932; *Sunday Dispatch*, 10 March 1935; and the *Sunday Mail*, 9 August 1936.

23. See Davies, 'Street gangs, crime and policing', pp. 251–68.

24. See the account of the Bridgeton Billy Boys, the largest of Glasgow's gangs, below.

25. On the contrasting patterns of gang formation in the South Side and East End of the city, see Davies, 'Street Gangs, Crime and Policing', pp. 254–5.

26. For broader treatments of sectarianism in Glasgow, see Murray, *Old Firm*; Tom Gallagher, *Glasgow: The Uneasy Peace: Religious Tension in Modern Scotland* (Manchester, 1987); and Damer, *Glasgow*.

27. Graham Walker, '"There's Not a Team like the Glasgow Rangers": Football and Religious Identity in Scotland', in Graham Walker and Tom Gallagher (eds.), *Sermons and Battle Hymns: Protestant Popular Culture in Modern Scotland* (Edinburgh, 1990), p. 158; idem, 'The Orange Order in Scotland between the Wars', *International Review of Social History* 37 (1992), pp. 176–206.

28. Walker, 'Orange Order', p. 187; Murray, *Old Firm*, pp. 154–6.

29. For a general account of the 12th of July parades, see Murray, *Old Firm*, pp. 154–6.

30. For a representative example, see the *Evening Citizen*, 13 July 1931.

31. See, for example, the *Evening Citizen*, 18 May 1931, 2 May 1932. For a detailed retrospective account of the violent disruption of a Catholic procession in the East End, see George Forbes and Paddy Meehan, *Such Bad Company: The Story of Glasgow Criminality* (Edinburgh, 1982), pp. 68–71.

32. For an account of an attack upon Celtic supporters arriving in the East End en route to the Celtic stadium, see the *Sunday Mail*, 6 March 1938.

33. See, for example, the case of Larry Rankin (pseud.), interviewed by Stephen Humphries for the BBC television series, *Forbidden Britain*, broadcast in 1994.

The tapes and transcript were deposited in the National Sound Archive at the British Library, video tape numbers C590/02/177–180.

34. *Weekly Record*, 11 December 1930.
35. *Evening Citizen*, 17 January 1955.
36. *Evening Citizen*, 17, 18 January 1955.
37. *Sunday Mail*, 10 July 1927.
38. *Evening Citizen*, 11 December 1930; *Weekly Record*, 20 December 1930; *Evening Citizen*, 17 January 1955.
39. *Evening Citizen*, 13 April 1931; *Glasgow Herald*, 23 August 1934, 17 March 1936; Colqhoun, *Life Begins at Midnight*, p. 18.
40. *Evening Citizen*, 18 January 1955.
41. *Weekly Record*, 20 December 1930, *Sunday Mail*, 10 July 1932.
42. *Evening Citizen*, 18 January 1955. In 1927, the U.S. Attorney's Office estimated that Al Capone's syndicate grossed approximately $105,000,000. See Laurence Bergreen, *Capone: The Man and the Era* (New York, 1996), p. 236.
43. *Evening Citizen*, 18 January 1955.
44. *Evening Citizen*, 18 January 1955.
45. *Bulletin*, 17 October 1931; *Evening Times*, 17 October 1931.
46. *Evening Citizen*, 31 October 1931, 26 January 1932.
47. *Evening Times*, 20 January 1932; *Evening Citizen*, 26 October 1932, 19 January 1955.
48. *Weekly Record*, 1 June 1929; *Evening Citizen*, 17 April 1930.
49. Sillitoe, *Cloak without Dagger*, p. 107.
50. See Murray, *Old Firm*, pp. 149–50, *Evening Citizen*, 4, 6, 7, 8 August 1930.
51. Sillitoe, *Cloak without Dagger*, pp. 127–33
52. Sillitoe, *Cloak without Dagger*, p. 129.
53. Sillitoe, *Cloak without Dagger*, p. 128.
54. Cockerill, *Sir Percy Sillitoe*, p. 141.
55. Cockerill, *Sir Percy Sillitoe*, pp. 143–4.
56. Sillitoe, *Cloak without Dagger*, p. 109; Cockerill, *Sir Percy Sillitoe*, pp. 107, 143.
57. Sillitoe, *Cloak without Dagger*, p. 110–11; Cockerill, *Sir Percy Sillitoe*, p. 107, 126–7, 143.
58. Cockerill, *Sir Percy Sillitoe*, pp. 132–3.
59. Cockerill, *Sir Percy Sillitoe*, pp. 147–8.
60. Cockerill, *Sir Percy Sillitoe*, p. 153.
61. Cockerill, *Sir Percy Sillitoe*, p. 143.
62. Davies, 'Street Gangs, Crime and Policing', pp. 262–4.
63. *Sunday Mail*, 4 March 1934, *Glasgow Herald*, 1 May 1934; Davies, 'Street Gangs, Crime and Policing', p. 265.
64. See, for example, the *Sunday Dispatch*, 10 March 1935.
65. The Walks in Scotland and Northern Ireland to commemorate the Battle of the Boyne were arranged for consecutive Saturdays, thus enabling the staunchest supporters of the Orange Order to attend both.
66. A.C. Hepburn, 'The Belfast Riots of 1935', *Social History* 15, 1 (1990), 75–96.
67. Hepburn, 'Belfast Riots', p. 83.
68. Hepburn, 'Belfast Riots', p. 84.
69. Hepburn, 'Belfast Riots', p. 80–2.
70. Alexander McArthur and H. Kingsley Long, *No Mean City* (London, 1935).
71. Seán Damer, 'No Mean Writer? The Curious case of Alexander McArthur', in Kevin McCarra and Hamish Whyte (eds.), *A Glasgow Collection: Essays in*

Honour of Joe Fisher (Glasgow, 1990), pp. 25–42; *Evening Citizen*, 28 October 1935.

72. Twenty-two special trains were laid on to convey the marchers to Airdrie, where the procession, three and a half miles long, took two hours to reach the rally at Bankhead Farm, *Sunday Mail*, 12 July 1936.
73. *Glasgow Herald*, 21 July 1936.
74. *Sunday Mail*, 9 August 1936.
75. Stewart gave an interview to the *Evening Citizen* on 12 August 1936 in which he told how he had received the letter the previous week.
76. *Sunday Mail*, 9 August 1936.
77. For initial reports of the disturbance, see the *Glasgow Herald*; *Daily Record* and *Evening Citizen*, 8 August 1936.
78. *Glasgow Herald*, 8 August 1936.
79. *Evening Citizen*, 8 August 1936; *Glasgow Herald*, 10 August 1936.
80. *Evening Citizen*, 8 August 1936.
81. *Daily Record*, 8 August 1936.
82. *Daily Record*, 8 August 1936.
83. *Evening Citizen*, 8 August 1936.
84. *Daily Record*, 11 August 1936.
85. *Sunday Mail*, 9 August 1936.
86. *Daily Record*, 10 August 1936.
87. *Glasgow Herald*; *Daily Record*, 11 August 1936.
88. *Evening Citizen*, 11 August 1936.
89. *Glasgow Herald*, 12, 13 August 1936; *Evening Citizen*, 12 August 1936.
90. *Evening Citizen*, 12 August 1936.
91. *Evening Times*, 12 August 1936.
92. See, for example, the case of John Mullin of Shanley Boys, *Evening Citizen*, 14 August 1936.
93. *Evening Times*, 17 August 1936.
94. *Glasgow Herald*, 18 August 1936.
95. *Glasgow Herald*, 20 August 1936.
96. *Glasgow Herald*, 20 August 1936.
97. Fullerton told in 1955 how the Billy Boys had been hired to break up Communist meetings, and as Bill Murray has noted, it is at least feasible that the gang's sponsors included the West of Scotland Economic League. See Murray, *Old Firm*, p. 157.
98. *Evening Citizen*, 24 August 1936.
99. *Evening Times*, 1 September 1936; *Glasgow Herald*, 2 September 1936.
100. *Glasgow Herald*, 15 September 1936.
101. *Evening Times*, 14 September 1936; *Glasgow Herald*, 15 September 1936.
102. *Glasgow Herald*, 16 September 1936.
103. *Evening Times*, 14 September 1936; *Glasgow Herald*, 15 September 1936.
104. *Evening Times*, 17 September 1936; *Glasgow Herald*, 18 September 1936.
105. Scottish Record Office, SC36/57/19, Glasgow Sheriff Court, Roll Book of Criminal and Quasi-Criminal Cases, case no. 5553; *Evening Times*, 22 September 1936; *Glasgow Herald*, 23 September 1936.
106. *Glasgow Herald*, 23 September 1936.
107. Sillitoe, *Cloak without Dagger*, pp. 130–31.
108. Sillitoe, *Cloak without Dagger*, p.131.
109. Sillitoe, *Cloak without Dagger*, p.131.

110. *Evening Citizen*, 23 September 1936.
111. It is possible that the magistrates' appeal to the local press to refrain from giving 'undue publicity' to the gangs may have served to obscure the full extent of anti-police feeling in late August and September 1936.
112. Sillitoe reordered events involving the Billy Boys and the Derry Boys, claiming, for example that an incident which place on 7 February 1931 occurred *after* the confrontation between the police and the Derry Boys on 7 August 1936. Compare Sillitoe, *Cloak without Dagger*, pp. 131–3 with the *Evening Citizen*, 7, 8 April 1931. Sillitoe further claimed that the sentences imposed upon three 'gangsters' at the High Court in Glasgow on 3 April 1935 for the murder of John McNamee sounded the 'knell of gangsterdom in Glasgow', *Cloak without Dagger*, pp. 133–5. However, in order to sustain this assertion, Sillitoe was forced to imply that the police ambush of the Billy Boys on 7 August 1936 took place prior to McNamee's murder.
113. Davies, 'Street Gangs, Crime and Policing', p. 266.
114. *Glasgow Herald*, 26 October 1936; *Reynolds News*, 20 December 1936.
115. See the comments by Larry Rankin, National Sound Archive, C590/02/177–180. Those who did 'tackle' police officers could earn a near legendary status in working-class districts such as Bridgeton or the Gorbals. See the account of Dan Cronin of the Beehive Boys in Davies, 'Street Gangs, Crime and Policing'.
116. Damer, *Glasgow*, p. 149.
117. See the editorial on 'Glasgow's Gangsters' in the *Evening Citizen*, 24 August 1936.
118. For trenchant critiques of the 'golden age' thesis, see Jerry White, 'Police and People in London in the 1930s', *Oral History* 11, 2 (1983), pp. 34–41; idem, *Worst Street in North London*; and Brogden, *On the Mersey Beat*. For a further discussion of relations between the police and the working classes in Glasgow, see Andrew Davies, *Street Gangs and Violence in Glasgow in the 1920s and 1930s* (Edinburgh, forthcoming).

4

The People's Police and the Miners of Saalfeld, August 1951

Richard Bessel

At the core of policing lies a fundamental contradiction: a police force exists both to uphold the political and social order as defined by the state which employs it and to protect the general public in whose name modern states usually claim legitimacy for their rule. In the day-to-day routine of policing this generally poses no great problem, at least in democratic political systems: the majority of the public tend to look to the police for protection against crime and to enforce a system of law which is widely regarded as legitimate. However, civil disorder which the police are either in no position to control or which the behaviour of the police actually provokes and/or exacerbates remains a disturbingly common feature of modern policing. Few police forces are completely immune from the problem, which may be inherent in the policing task itself. Despite being exercised within vastly differing social and economic structures, sets of cultural assumptions, administrative structures, governmental systems and ideologies guiding policy and action, policing in various contexts tends to have the following in common: a general popular acceptance of the day-to-day policing role, and the occasional instance of rioting and violent conflict between the police and disaffected groups within society.

Essentially, it appears that the following conditions are required for major disturbances and conflict to develop between the police and the public:

1. There is a prehistory of minor incidents, harassment and mis-understanding between the police and particular groups among the civil population.
2. The groups which either present or are seen to present a major challenge to public order have a strong sense of their own identity as separate from, and generally antagonistic to, the general population.
3. The groups which present a challenge to public order do not accept the legitimacy of the police in their role as enforcers of law and order.
4. The groups which present a challenge to public order have, in the eyes of government authorities and in the media, essentially been stigmatised and their concerns and grievances dismissed as illegitimate.
5. The police have not, in the main, been recruited from among the group or groups which present a major challenge to their authority.
6. The police have failed to develop adequate tactics and/or are insufficiently trained and equipped to deal with major outbreaks of civil unrest.
7. The police, at least initially, do not have sufficient force at their disposal to contain the unrest and prevent its escalation into a major incident.
8. A major concern of the police lies in saving face and demon-strating that they can maintain control of public space and the respect of the public.

In this schema overt politics is conspicuous by its absence, how-ever, and it can be tempting to examine such disturbance as an essentially tactical problem, with its roots (and likely solutions) lying in the tactics police forces employ when dealing with the public and particularly with alienated groups.

This article aims to test the extent to which the general conditions and patterns of conflict between police and public may be shaped by overt political pressures, and does so by looking at the early history of a quite extraordinary police force: the East German *Volks-polizei* (People's Police). The *Volkspolizei* was a force which in its composition, its purpose and its mode of operation was explicitly political from the outset, and one which on occasion in its early years faced massive popular hostility and unrest.[1] When *Volks-polizei* was established in the Soviet Occupation Zone of Germany after the Second World War, it consisted almost entirely of people who had had neither previous experience in police uniform nor police training – a consequence of the determination of German Communists and Soviet occupiers to make a radical break with the Nazi past as well as to the lack of training facilities. In the immediate postwar period, it was confronted with a huge wave of violent and property crime, which in the economic and social chaos following the collapse of Nazi Germany (and with marauding Soviet soldiers) was many times prewar levels. Yet initially it was remarkably ill-equipped to deal with such enormous problems: it lacked adequate communications equipment, motor transport, weaponry and often even adequate clothing. And this was a police force which was conceived of in explicitly political terms, whose personnel from the outset had been chosen largely according to political criteria, which especially from 1948 onwards had been purged repeatedly of allegedly politically unreliable elements and disciplined by 'Political-Culture Sections', and which viewed its purpose and activities in overtly political terms. A senior officer of the Thuringian *Schutzpolizei* put it succinctly while reviewing police work at a conference in late December 1949 in Weimar: 'Police work is Party work. One cannot separate these terms. Every member of the *Volkspolizei* is a Party worker and every officer of the *Volkspolizei* is a functionary of the Party.'[2]

It was this police force which formed the young East German communist regime's first line of defence when popular discontent erupted in June 1953 in a workers' uprising – an uprising which threatened the very survival of the young German Democratic Republic (GDR) and was suppressed only with the employment of overwhelming force by the Soviet Army and at the cost of many lives.[3] The 'People's Police' often were the targets of popular anger in June 1953, particularly as crowds attempted to free (political) prisoners and attacked those whose job it was to guard police gaols.[4] The eruption of 17 June 1953 marked a milestone in the history of the GDR, but it was not the first instance in which East German workers rose up against state authority and directed their anger against the People's Police. During the late 1940s and early 1950s the *Volkspolizei* repeatedly fell into conflict with the population, in particular with the uranium miners of the Wismut AG in Saxony and Thuringia. This posed problems of a quite fundamental nature for the new communist political elites of East Germany, not least because they regarded themselves as governing in the name and interests of the working class. Yet here – in large measure due to demands imposed by the Soviet occupying power to whom the East German communists owed political allegiance – a major component of that working class had shown itself to be, to put it mildly, not terribly appreciative of the efforts which the new workers' state was making on their behalf. When conflict erupted and the political ideology of the new regime was brutally challenged by the actions of precisely those people in whose name that regime supposedly governed, at the sharp end stood the People's Police. The result was probably the most serious single confrontation between the East German People's Police and the East German people before the 1953 uprising: the riots in Saalfeld in August 1951.[5]

The mining industry in the Soviet Occupation Zone of Germany (to 1949) and then the German Democratic Republic was concentrated in its southern *Länder*. In addition to the traditional brown-coal mining areas in Saxony and Sachsen-Anhalt, which had been centres of working-class radicalism and unrest during the early years of the Weimar Republic, a huge new mining industry was established after the Second World War in western Saxony and eastern Thuringia, where uranium had been discovered. In 1947, as part of the reparations programme, a 'Soviet Joint-Stock Company', the Wismut AG, was set up under the direct control of the Soviet secret police to mine uranium for the USSR atomic weapons development programme.[6] Tens of thousands of workers were brought to southwestern Saxony and eastern Thuringia to mine uranium, either drafted in as forced labourers, punished as criminals, or induced to volunteer by promises of good working and living conditions and high salaries. Initially the new miners were brought in from the large Saxon cities (Dresden, Leipzig, Chemnitz, Zwickau), but as the Soviet demand for labour at Wismut grew they were recruited from further afield, including the northernmost (and largely rural) Land of Mecklenburg and straight out of the reception camps at Frankfurt/Oder set up for men returning from Soviet prisoner-of-war camps. Tens of thousands of often untrained workers, many in poor health, were compelled to mine uranium in primitive conditions, digging with pick-axes and often working knee-deep in radioactive slime, without adequate clothing or medical care. Norman Naimark, in his excellent study, *The Russians in Germany*, has described Wismut as 'a German Kolyma of sorts … created in the Erzgebirge, with forced labour brought into the region and subjected to humiliating and unbearable physical circumstances'.[7]

With tens of thousands of newly recruited miners suddenly descending on the Wismut region, the population of the district of

Aue, the central distribution point for Wismut workers, nearly doubled between 1946 and 1951. Consequently, housing the new miners was an acute problem – at a time when, due to the wartime bombings and the postwar influx of German refugees ('resettlers' in the official language of the GDR) from east of the new border along the Oder-Neiße,[8] housing already was extremely scarce. Local people were not keen to offer Wismut miners private rooms, and the recruits were often housed in barracks and tents, schools and factory buildings.[9] And since the Wismut operation was run by the Soviet Ministry of Internal Affairs, which was concerned to exploit German uranium resources regardless of the effects which this might have on the German communities involved or the policing thereof,[10] there was little that the German Communist leadership (or even the Soviet Military Administration for that matter) could do about the awful conditions in which the new workers were compelled to live and work. The result was the rapid build-up of a large, ill-housed, disaffected male work force, which because of the relatively high wages paid to those who had volunteered for work in the Wismut mines, had a fair amount of money to spend on drink and prostitutes and were not well disposed towards representatives of the new political order. This constellation in turn led to considerable tensions between the Wismut miners and the local population of towns suddenly inundated with thousands of rowdy and unwelcome newcomers.

The sudden introduction of the huge new and disaffected Wismut work force obviously created serious problems for the police, who were faced repeatedly with public disturbances involving the uranium miners. Not surprisingly, the Wismut workers were regarded as a major threat to law and order and to public security by the *Volkspolizei*, one for which special tactics needed to be developed. In December 1948, at a conference of leaders of the Saxon *Schutzpolizei* in Glauchau (west of Chemnitz, and also in the Wismut region), the head of the District Police Office (*Kreispolizeiamt*, KPA) in Aue discussed the 'alarm plan' that the *Volkspolizei* in his district had developed in order to respond to unrest among Wismut miners. There, it was said, the *Volkspolizei* already had initiated a plan that involved the mobilisation of between 150 and 200 men 'in order to proceed against this reactionary section of the miners and thereby to improve the standing of the police in their eyes'. According to the plan, when the head of the KPA gave the alarm, the police would gather, have orders for raids and for police beats to hand, and have the necessary motor vehicles at their disposal ready for use. Nevertheless, the District Police Chief admitted that some fundamental problems in the relations between the miners and the police remained:

> Again and again we have attempted to win over these miners through political enlightenment, but always in vain. For these reactionary, fascist elements the police are like a red rag to a bull and [the police] can only take rigorous action when they appear en masse [as] a minority would simply be bludgeoned. In our area a well-functioning alarm plan is therefore of special importance.[11]

The relations between miners and police throughout western Saxony during the late 1940s and in southeastern Thuringia during the early 1950s, once the numbers of Wismut miners had mushroomed there too as the Wismut operation expanded westward into Thuringia, were similar. What appears to have been lacking throughout the expanded regions, however, was a 'well-functioning alarm plan'.

The social problems created by the growth of the Wismut operation, the understandable disaffection of its work force and the inadequacies of the police erupted in August 1951 in the small Thuringian city of Saalfeld, about 40 kilometres south of Weimar. In a sense, one might almost regard the outburst of violence in Saalfeld as inevitable. For one thing, tempers in and around Saalfeld were particularly frayed in the summer of 1951, as a large number of new Wismut recruits had been transferred to southeastern Thuringia in mid-June – exacerbating an already critical housing situation and heightening the already substantial tensions in the region.[12] As one officer pointed out to a conference of the Thuringian *Volkspolizei* leadership gathered to discuss the violence in Saalfeld soon after the incident, the shift of the Wismut operation from Saxony into Thuringia had 'caused considerable disquiet among the population'.[13] For another, not only had a general climate of tension and mutual hostility developed between the *Volkspolizei* and the workers of the Wismut region, where the police viewed the miners as a dangerous threat to public order and the miners viewed the police as the public face of an unjust and oppressive system, but the Saalfeld riot was not the first violent confrontation involving Wismut miners. For example, not long before in the town of Oberschlema, from which many of the miners in Saalfeld had been transferred in mid-June, police and miners had confronted one another at the railway station, with the police employing water cannon and the workers responding with stones.[14] And just a few days before the big Saalfeld riots, on the evening of 13–14 August, a fight in nearby Rudolstadt between drunken Wismut workers and members of the Free German Youth organisation, had led to the arrest of four Wismut miners.[15] However, the most serious incident was probably that which had occurred two years earlier in Zwickau, where by the summer of 1949 there already were 90,000 miners in the district with many more expected.

In many respects the violence which erupted in Zwickau in the late summer of 1949 prefigured that which occurred two years later in Saalfeld.[16] Tensions resulting from the dreadful conditions in which the miners worked and lived combined with an ill-judged police response to provoke serious violence. Angry, tired and hungry miners returning from their shifts in vastly overcrowded trains to the western Saxon city of Zwickau, where they invariably found the shops empty of food, pulled the emergency brake, climbed onto the roofs and running-boards of the railway carriages as well as onto the locomotive, and 'carried on as they wanted'. An attempt by a small band of 20 policemen to bring hundreds of unruly miners to order succeeded only in provoking confrontation. Miners armed with their tools attacked the police, who then tried to rescue threatened and wounded comrades first with police dogs and then by firing warning shots. This caused the crowd to rise up against the police 'like a typhoon', attack a police station, smash its windows and front door, and demand that the police 'hand over the policemen who had fired shots so that lynch justice in the American style could be applied'. Fortunately for the policeman who had fired the offending shots, the miners in fact disarmed and turned him over to a Soviet officer. However, the message was clear: the People's Police had turned a tense situation into a major violent incident. Passing his judgement on this failure to deal with the unruly miners, the head of the *Polit-Kultur* section of the Zwickau police admitted 'that the *Volkspolizei* has too little contact with the colliers, with the proletarians of the mining industry'.[17] This response was typical not only in its vocabulary but also in the subsequent lack of any effective attempt to turn these words into deeds: two summers later the *Volkspolizei* obviously still had not managed to build up satisfactory 'contact with the colliers'.

As with so many violent confrontations between police and people, the Saalfeld riot was triggered by a relatively minor but representative incident.[18] Shortly after 17:00 on the evening of Thursday, 16 August 1951, a man appeared at the local police station, bleeding profusely from one of his arms; he claimed that drunken Wismut miners were harassing members of the public and had cut him with a broken beer bottle. Three police officers were sent out to the Market Square, where they saw four drunken Wismut miners fighting amongst themselves and threatening passers-by, and moved to take one of the miners, who had injured a member of the public, into custody. According to police reports, the miner resisted arrest and kicked one of the policemen, and consequently had to be taken by force (being hit on the chin) to the police station at the other end of the square. Soon about thirty people, mostly Wismut workers, had gathered around the police station to 'express solidarity' with the arrested man, to protest against his arrest and to demand his release. Insults were hurled at the police, and two further miners, both drunk, were arrested.

Outside the police station the crowd grew larger, and soon roughly 300 people had gathered shouting 'release our comrades' (*gebt unsere Kumpels heraus*). At this point another Wismut miner, who had been prominent in calling for the crowd not to return to work for their shift but instead to free by force those in custody, was arrested. The crowd continued to grow, as miners collected their comrades from the local pubs. According to police accounts, two women (who were also Wismut workers, and who were arrested the following day) were particularly effective in stirring up popular anger against the police, shouting among other things, 'Beat the pigs, the bastards to death, get our four Wismut-comrades out' (*Schlägt die Schweine, die Lumpen tot, holt unsere 4 Wismuth-Kumpels heraus*). A Soviet officer appeared together with an interpreter and tried to calm the crowd, but without success. It was now about 21:30, when three dozen police reinforcements arrived from a nearby pit (raising the total at the station to about 50) and were threatened by miners with pickaxes. By this time the *Volkspolizei* leadership in the Thuringian capital of Weimar had become involved. From 20:00 onwards the police in the Saalfeld station were in telephone contact with the Land headquarters in Weimar, having made what one officer later described as 'police SOS calls'.[19] The police in Saalfeld were ordered not to fire on the crowd, an order subsequently repeated by the head of the Thuringian Criminal Police, *Inspekteur* Zahmel, who stipulated that under no circumstances were the police to use their firearms; and *Volkspolizei-Inspekteur* Opadlik from the central headquarters in Berlin ordered that, given the increasingly threatening situation, the four arrested miners be released.

However, by this time it was too late. With the release of the arrested men the assembled crowd sensed that it had gained the upper hand; and with a change in shift, yet more miners, convinced that the police had arrested and mishandled more of their comrades, arrived and made the crowd even larger. The police allowed a delegation of miners to come into the station house, to demonstrate to the crowd that no further miners were being held prisoner; however, when the miners emerged to confirm this the crowd refused to believe them and instead threw stones through the windows of the police headquarters and smashed the front door. At that point about fifty miners managed to enter the building through the broken windows, looking for arrested comrades. They got upstairs and proceeded to smash more windows. The police inside the station had completely lost control of the situation.[20] Zahmel and Opadlik called for reinforcements, and motorised units from the surrounding area were dispatched to Saalfeld. By the time Opadlik himself had arrived at the scene together with Zahmel, at about 23:00 to a chorus of stones and shouts of 'Beat the Volkspolizei Dogs Dead' (*Schlägt die Hunde der Volkspolizei tot*), the number of miners demonstrating in front of the police station had grown to over 400. Accompanied by a Soviet officer, Opadlik tried, with some success, to calm the crowd on the Market Square by promising that any police officers guilty of improper behaviour towards the arrested miners would be called to account. However, provocateurs in the crowd shouted demands that the 'guilty officers' responsible for the arrests be handed over so that the crowd could 'punish them ourselves'.

At that moment, a squad of armed motorised police arrived on the scene. The sight of armed police further enraged the crowd, members of which attacked the police with pickaxes and miners lamps, pulled them off their motorcycles and took their weapons. Within the police headquarters about 100 demonstrators reached the upstairs of the building and proceeded to smash up the furniture, steal clothing, destroy the telephone exchange and roam the building in search of policemen whom they asserted they wanted to beat to death. Once the station had fallen into the control of the miners, 'in order to avoid unnecessary losses' (as a police report subsequently put it) the police abandoned the building, fleeing through windows or climbing onto the roof. According to one report, the number of people amassed around the police station reached 800; according to another, altogether 3,000 people had gathered between 22:00 and 23:00, including 800–1,000 Wismut workers armed with pit lamps and pickaxes.[21] Some of the demonstrators then marched off towards the prison attached to the local court, forced open the prison gates and, after threatening to hang the policeman on duty, freed two more miners who had been arrested earlier on unrelated charges. The local fire station and the municipal hospital also were threatened. It was not until after 2:00 in the morning of the seventeenth that the miners left the police station and the crowd dispersed, and the police were able to start clearing up the damage, repair broken windows and get the offices back into some semblance of order. By the time the dust had settled, one police motorcycle had been stolen, a police car had been badly damaged, and two police officers had suffered serious head wounds; total damage to the police station in Saalfeld was estimated at 25,000 Marks.[22] An inventory of the damage caused at the police station listed roughly 100 panes of glass broken, 20 damaged typewriters, 40 damaged doors, 30 smashed tables, 30 destroyed lights and a number of broken lockers.[23]

While all this had been going on, the local police leadership, realising that things had got out of hand, tried desperately to contact their superiors in Berlin: the Deputy Chief of the *Volkspolizei* Willi Seifert (who in 1961 would be a member of the Staff of the National Defence Council responsible for building the Berlin Wall) and People's Police Chief Karl Maron. (It was not until about 1:00 in the morning that Seifert and Maron were reached.) Calls went out for all available police from the surrounding region to come to Saalfeld;[24] police reserves blocked the streets leading into the town. On the following day the First Secretary of the Thuringian Socialist Unity Party Erich Mückenberger, the Thuringian Interior Minister Willy Gebhardt, the head (*Chef-Inspekteur*) of the Volkspolizei in Thuringia Georg König and the head of the area State Security (MfS, Secret Police) Menzel, arrived in Saalfeld. Gebhardt made a short speech on the Market Square, but was shouted down by Wismut workers and local shopkeepers. He also met with representatives of the Soviet Control Commission for Thuringia as well as of the *Volkspolizei* to discuss how to keep the lid on in Saalfeld. The ruling Socialist Unity Party also mobilised its membership, 'concentrating' large numbers of party members (1500 according to one report, some hundreds of 'agitators' according to another) from other towns in Saalfeld, in order 'enlighten' the population in the Market Square.[25] A local incident sparked by a drunken miner had escalated to the point that the national leadership of the East German police and the leading politicians in Thuringia became involved.

Throughout the following day rumours circulated that further trouble was brewing. On the evening of the seventeenth, *Volks-*

polizei headquarters in Berlin reported that, according to 'confidential sources', something like 3,000 Wismut workers were planning to demonstrate. Allegedly the miners had heard rumours that sixteen of their colleagues had been arrested and were determined to set them free. According to the information reaching Berlin an 'illegal uprising leadership' had been formed.[26] (The alleged plan was to attack other buildings, including shops in the town, in order to create diversions before storming the police headquarters.) In fact things quieted down fairly quickly in Saalfeld without force having to be used. The rumours, it would appear, were largely a reflection of the paranoia of the police and of the difficulties involved in gathering reliable information about popular sentiment in a society where the press and other expressions of public opinion were tightly controlled.

The *Volkspolizei*'s own subsequent evaluation of the confrontation attested to the fact that it had been a disaster for police-community relations. However, this is not to say that the miners who attacked the police station in Saalfeld enjoyed widespread popular support or were regarded as a working-class vanguard against an oppressive regime or police state. (Nevertheless, it is noteworthy that many people who were not Wismut miners joined the crowd outside the police station and helped to storm the prison and the police station; indeed, at the high point of the trouble probably only about one third of the three thousand participants were miners.) Ever since the region had become inundated with often unruly Wismut workers, and unpleasant confrontations (the shoving of pedestrians on the pavements, fights with drunken miners, the breaking of windows) between Wismut miners and local people became a daily occurrence, the local population had looked anxiously to the *Volkspolizei* for protection.[27] The tensions and hostility between the incoming miners and the native population, between disruptive and alienated (but relatively well-paid) miners and the local citizenry, were greatly amplified by the violence of August 1951, as was the dissatisfaction with the apparent inability of the police to keep the peace and protect the population. In the words of Georg König, the head of the *Volkspolizei* in Thuringia, 'the prestige of the Police in Saalfeld has been severely shaken, if it has not disappeared'.[28] Commenting on the 'morale of the population' in the wake of the incident, the Thuringian *Volkspolizei* noted in a lengthy report on the Saalfeld rioting: 'In the opinion of the population the *Volkspolizei* must intervene in a fierce and unmistakable manner, so that further riots of a small portion of the Wismut workers are nipped in the bud.' The report concluded that the prestige of the *Volkspolizei* in Thuringia had taken a severe beating, both within the *Volkspolizei* itself and among the public at large.[29]

In another report about the Saalfeld incident, the *Volkspolizei* leadership in Berlin noted that the public at large discussed the riots intensively and believed 'that such a vacillating *Volkspolizei* guarantees no safeguard for the population'. Furthermore, it was reported, 'the members of the [Saalfeld *Volkspolizei*] are severely depressed and argue that under no circumstances should the police leave rioters to their own devices in future, even if that means the utilisation of all available means including the use of firearms'. For the time being, the Berlin leadership concluded, the *Volkspolizei* had to reckon that any attempt to arrest Wismut workers for breaking the law was liable to result in their being violently set free.[30] It was altogether a rather depressing assessment of ability of the People's Police to enforce the law and deal with the German people.

If these reports are accurate, the violence in Saalfeld and popular reactions to it appear to have had many similarities with violent confrontations between police and people in countries with very different political systems. Neither the fact that the *Volkspolizei* were serving a dictatorial communist state in a divided nation and were ultimately backed by the armed forces of the Soviet Union, nor the peculiarities of the working and living conditions of the Wismut work force appear to have made the patterns of provocation and violence fundamentally different from those elsewhere. Instead, it would appear that both the Saalfeld upheaval itself and the reactions to it were typical of situations in which an inadequately trained and understrength police force with a history of perceived brutality confront an alienated and violent crowd. The majority of the local population wanted protection from a threatening and unruly group, and were angered when the police proved unable to provide that protection; and the police on the ground felt let down and undermined by their leadership, which they held responsible for tactical failures. In this regard at least, policing in the German Democratic Republic during its early years does not appear to have been all that different from policing in other (pluralist, capitalist) societies and political systems.

It is clear that the events in Saalfeld were taken extremely seriously by the leadership of the People's Police, both in Thuringia and throughout the German Democratic Republic. In the immediate aftermath of the upheaval, 'sixty physically strong, politically reliable' policemen were gathered from other stations and transferred permanently to Saalfeld, and a motorised squad of thirty-four men also was stationed in city.[31] Furthermore, the *Volkspolizei* leadership ordered that a number of measures be taken throughout the GDR to prevent a recurrence of what happened in Saalfeld. The measures were a predictable mixture of tactical moves to strengthen the capability of the police to ward off or suppress outbursts of popular violence, and included the following: All district police offices were to have guard posts at their entrance, and these were now to be supplied with alarm bells; police stations in the Wismut region in Thuringia and Saxony, near the border with West Berlin and near the Demarcation Line with West Germany, were to have their doors and windows strengthened and where necessary supplied with metal bars; and in these sensitive areas motorised 'guard battalions' (*Wachbataillione*) were to be set up as soon as possible and the Border Police formations were to be strengthened; and every police station was to have a guard dog for night duty.[32]

The ways in which the *Volkspolizei* assessed this and similar incidents were typical of how police forces generally respond when faced with violent challenges to their authority and to public order. There was no real attempt made to analyse critically what had happened in Saalfeld in August 1951, to question the relationship of the police or governmental system to the people in whose interests it was supposed to be acting. Yet the new political system was supposed to be building the foundations of socialism in the interests precisely of that group which had caused the disturbances: workers. Instead, the police leadership sought tactical improvements and more equipment. When it came to looking for the causes of the unrest, the explanations were couched in terms of conspiracy, provocateurs and outside agitators. It is difficult enough for police chiefs and politicians in pluralist societies to examine tactical failures in an open and critical manner; in a one-party state, which operated under the watchful eye of an occupying military power and which was dogmatically committed to a political ideology which ascribed certain characteristics to certain social groups regardless of the facts, it probably was impossible.

In October 1951 no less a figure than Karl Maron, the Chief of the *Volkspolizei* in the German Democratic Republic, wrote to Walter Ulbricht, General Secretary of the Socialist Unity Party, about the events in Saalfeld:

> It is apparent that the enemy is pursuing the tactic of exploiting any intervention by the *Volkspolizei*, no matter what the cause, for provo-

cations against the *Volkspolizei*, in order to bring the population into opposition to our democratic state and to reduce the authority of the state apparatus. A characteristic of most of these events is the worrying fact that the *Volkspolizei* is not being supported by the working population, and even members of the SED [Socialist Unity Party of Germany], the FDJ [Free German Youth] and other mass organisations behave in a completely passive or 'neutral' manner. ... This isolation of the *Volkspolizei* is very dangerous and absolutely must be eliminated.[33]

As became apparent with the uprising of June 1953, when the *Volkspolizei* again became the targets of popular anger (and a number were killed), the isolation of the People's Police from the people was not 'eliminated' and indeed remained 'very dangerous'. The introduction in late 1952 of a socialist model of community policing, whereby the entire GDR was divided into 'sections' each with a resident police officer (ABV, *Abschnittsbevollmächtigter*) responsible for the security and supervision of the local population, whatever its later successes,[34] failed to bridge the gulf between police and people in time. In a political system which precluded open discussion of the problems faced by a police organisation in its relations with the population, it probably was impossible completely to 'eliminate' the isolation of the police. The underlying causes of the Saalfeld violence – the dreadful working and living conditions of the Wismut miners (caused by the callous and exploitative behaviour of the Soviet authorities), and the fact that the political system was regarded widely as unjust and illegitimate, serving Soviet rather than German interests, could not be debated frankly in the closed dictatorial system of the German Democratic Republic. Whereas the tactical problems facing the *Volkspolizei* – which were confronted by hostile groups and whose misjudged responses provoked violence rather imposed order – were similar to those faced by many other police forces, the possible responses were circumscribed by political structures. In the end, the main path open to the East German authorities was to increase the scale and scope of the police apparatus. This they did. By the end of 1955 the *Volkspolizei* alone – not counting the members of the State Security organisation, the '*Volkspolizei* in barracks' (*Kasernierte Volkspolizei*) which became the National People's Army, and the Border Police – numbered almost 100,000 members[35] – as many as had been employed in the whole of the German Empire before 1914.[36]

Notes

1. On the early history of the Volkspolizei and the considerable problems which it faced, see Richard Bessel, 'Polizei zwischen Krieg und Sozialismus. Die Anfänge der Volkspolizei nach dem Zweiten Weltkrieg', in Christian Jansen, Lutz Niethammer, and Bernd Weisbrod (eds.), *Von der Aufgabe der Freiheit. Gesellschaft und Politik in Deutschland im 19. und 20. Jahrhundert. Festschrift für Hans Mommsen zum 5. November 1995* (Berlin, 1995), pp. 517–31; idem., 'Grenzen des Polizeistaates. Polizei und Gesellschaft in der SBZ und frühen DDR, 1945-1953', in Richard Bessel and Ralph Jessen (eds.), *Die Grenzen der Diktatur. Staat und Gesellschaft in der DDR* (Göttingen, 1996), pp. 224–52. For a good recent overview of the Volkspolizei from its beginnings after the Second World War until its demise once the GDR collapsed, see Thomas Lindenberger, 'Die Deutsche Volkspolizei (1945–1990)', in Torsten Diedrich, Hans Ehlert, and Rüdiger Wenzke (eds.), *Im Dienste der Partei. Handbuch der bewaffneten Organe der DDR* (Berlin, 1998), pp. 97–152.

2. Bundesarchiv (BA), DO-1-7, Nr. 266, ff. 152-69: Landesbehörde der Volkspolizei, Abteilung Schutzpolizei, 'Protokoll-Notiz über die am 28.12.1949 bei der LBdVP Thüringen stattgefundene Arbeitstagung der Leiter der S[chutzpolizei]', Weimar, 28 Dec. 1949 (report by VP-Inspekteur Dams).

3. The best recent histories of the uprising of 17 June 1953 are to be found in Torsten Diedrich, *Der 17. Juni 1953 in der DDR* (Berlin, 1991); and Ilko-Sascha Kowalczuk, Armin Mitter and Stefan Wolle (eds.), *Der Tag X – 17. Juni 1953. Die "Innere Staatsgründung" der DDR als Ergebnis der Krise 1952/54* (Berlin, 1995).

4. BA, DO-1-11, Nr. 1126, ff. 101-15: untitled report, Berlin, 22 June 1953.

5. For a pioneering account and analysis of the Saalfeld incident, focusing on the attitudes and living conditions of the miners and on forms of social protest rather than on the tactics of the police, see Andrew Port, 'When Workers Rumbled: the Wismut Upheaval of August 1951 in East Germany', *Social History* 22, 2 (May 1997), pp. 139–73. See also Heide Roth and Torten Diedrich, 'Wir sind Kumpel – uns kann keiner. Der 17. Juni 1953 in der SAG Wismut', in Rainer Karlsch and Harm Schröter (eds.), *"Strahlende Vergangenheit". Studien zur Geschichte des Uranbergbaus der Wismut* (St. Katharinen, 1996), pp. 228–59. Comprehensive police reports and analysis of the incident may be found in BA, DO-1-11, Nr. 8, and Thüringisches Hauptstaatsarchiv Weimar (ThHStA) Landesbehörde de Volkspolizei (LBdVP), Bestand 5, Nr. 29.

6. See Reimar Paul, *Das Wismut Erbe. Geschichte und Folgen des Uranbergbaus in Thüringen und Sachsen* (Göttingen, 1991), pp. 11–61; Rainer Karsch, *Allein bezahlt? Die Reparationsleistungen der SBZ/DDR 1945–1953* (Berlin, 1993), pp. 136–50; Norman Naimark, *The Russians in Germany, The History of the Soviet Zone of Occupation, 1945–1949* (Cambridge, Mass., 1995), pp. 238–48; Rainer Karlsch and Harm Schröter (eds.), *"Strahlende Vergangenheit". Studien zur Geschichte des Uranbergbaus der Wismut* (St. Katharinen, 1996).

7. Naimark, *The Russians in Germany*, p. 239.

8. Roughly a quarter of the population of the Saalfeld district in January 1947 consisted of 'resettlers'. See Port, 'When Workers Rumbled', pp. 150.

9. Port, 'When Workers Rumbled', pp. 150-1.

10. According to the head of the Thuringian Volkspolizei, Georg König, a Soviet officer representing Wismut let it be known that it was of secondary importance if

a tavern were smashed up, 'but it is bad if half a shift of production is lost'. See ThHStA, LBdVP, Bestand 5, Nr. 29, f. 7: Landesbehörde der Volkspolizei Thüringen, 'Aktennotiz über einen kurzen Bericht des Chefinspekteurs König an das Sekretariat der Landesleitung der Partei am 23.9.51', Weimar, 23 August 1951.

11. BA, DO-1-7, Nr. 265, ff. 66–70: Landespolizeibehörde, 'Protokoll über die Arbeitstagung der Schutzpolizei in Glauchau am 15.12.48', Dresden, 16 December 1948.

12. Port, 'When Workers Rumbled', pp. 151–2.

13. ThHStA, LBdVP, Bestand 5, Nr. 29, ff. 8–13 (here f. 8): 'Tagung vom 25.8.51 in der LBdVP. Diskussion'.

14. Paul, *Das Wismut Erbe*, pp. 24–6; Port, 'When Workers Rumbled', p. 157.

15. ThHStA, LBdVP, Bestand 5, Nr. 29, f. 2: Landesbehörde der Volkspolizei Thüringen, Operativstab, to the HVDVP, Operativstab, Weimar, 15 August 1951.

16. The Zwickau confrontation was discussed at length, in the presence of Walter Ulbricht and Volkspolizei Chief Kurt Fischer, at a conference of 'Polit-Kultur' leaders in Berlin in September 1949. See BA, DO-1-7, Nr. 102, ff. 1–234: 'Stenographische Niederschrift über die PK-Leiter Konferenz am 8. und 9. September 1949 der Deutschen Verwaltung des Innern in Berlin-Niederschönhausen, Seckendorferstr. 31' (esp. the reports of the unnamed 'PK-Leiter der Inspektion II, Zwickau' and Kommandeur Kalbe of the Zwickau Volkspolizei, ff. 176–83).

17. BA, DO-1-7, Nr. 102, f. 176.

18. BA, DO-1-11, Nr. 8, f. 24: Hauptabteilung K, 'Tel. Durchsage von VP-Insp. Opadlik am 16.8.51, um 22.45 Uhr'; BA, DO-1-11, Nr. 8, ff. 27–30: HV Deutsche Volkspolizei, 'Überfall auf das VPKA Saalfeld', Berlin, 17 August 1951; BA, DO-1-11, Nr. 8, ff. 37–45: 'Bericht über die im Auftrag des Chefs durchgeführte Untersuchung über die Ursachen der Vorkommnisse im VPKA Saalfeld, in der Nacht vom 16. zum 17.8.51'; ThHStA, LBdVP, Bestand 5, Nr. 29, ff. 8–13: 'Tagung vom 25.8.51 in der LBdVP. Discussion'; Port, 'When Workers Rumbled'.

19. ThHStA, LBdVP, Bestand 5, Nr. 29, ff. 8–13 (here f. 9): 'Tagung vom 25.8.51 in der LBdVP. Diskussion'.

20. BA, DO-1-11, Nr. 8, f. 25: 'Anruf des VP-Insp. Odpadlik [sic]', Berlin, 17 August 1951. According to Opadlik, the Volkspolizei leadership in the station 'completely lost its head', and the local commanders either had retreated to their offices or were nowhere to be found.

21. For the second estimate, BA, DO-1-11, Nr. 8, ff. 76–80: Volkspolizeikreisamt Saalfeld, Sekretariat, 'Bericht über die Vorkommnisse im und vor dem Volkspolizeikreisamt in Saalfeld am 16. und 17. 1951', Saalfeld, 28 August 1951.

22. BA, DO-1-11, Nr. 8, ff. 32–4: Hauptabteilung K – Abteilung C, 'Besondere Vorkommnisse in Saalfeld nach dem Stand vom 18.8.1951 02,00 Uhr', Berlin, 18 August 1951

23. BA, DO-1-11, Nr. 8, ff. 72–4: HVDVP – Operativstab, 'Ergänzungsbericht zu den Vorkommnissen in Saalfeld', Berlin, 18 August 1951.

24. In addition to the police from Saalfeld itself, on 18 August there were 130 men from the HVA-Bereitschaft (tactical police force) in Gera (about 40 kilometres to the northeast), 30 men from the special tactical force (Einsatzkommando) of the headquarters (LBdVP) of the Thuringian Volkspolizei, and 120 men from various police stations in Erfurt, Jena, Gera and Weimar. See BA, DO-1-11, Nr. 8, ff. 72–4: HVDVP – Operativstab, 'Ergänzungsbericht zu den Vorkommnissen in Saalfeld', Berlin, 18 August 1951.

25. BA, DO-1-11, Nr. 8, f. 26: Hauptabteilung K, 'Lage in Saalfeld am 17.8.51, 17.45 Uhr', Berlin, 17 August 1951; BA, DO-1-11, Nr. 8, ff. 37–45: 'Bericht über die im Auftrag des Chefs durchgeführte Untersuchung über die Ursachen der Vorkommnisse im VPKA Saalfeld, in der Nacht vom 16. zum 17.8.51'.

26. BA, DO-1-11, Nr. 8, f. 26: Hauptabteilung K, 'Lage in Saalfeld am 17.8.51, 17.45 Uhr', Berlin, 17 August 1951.

27. ThHStA, LBdVP, Bestand 5, Nr. 29, ff. 8–13 (here f. 8): 'Tagung vom 25.8.51 in der LBdVP. Discussion'.

28. ThHStA, LBdVP, Bestand 5, Nr. 29, f. 7: Landesbehörde der Volkspolizei Thüringen, 'Aktennotiz über einen kurzen Bericht des Chefinspekteurs König an das Sekretariat der Landesleitung der Partei am 23.9.51', Weimar, 23 August 1951.

29. The report's conclusions were: 1) The confidence of the members of the Saalfeld Volkspolizei in the police leadership, above all in the police leadership of the LBdVP [Land Authority of the Volkspolizei], has been shaken; and 2.) The confidence of the population of the city of Saalfeld in the Volkspolizei itself has been shaken as well. See BA, DO-1-11, Nr. 8, ff. 37–45: 'Bericht über die im Auftrag des Chefs durchgeführte Untersuchung über die Ursachen der Vorkommnisse im VPKA Saalfeld, in der Nacht vom 16. zum 17.8.51'.

30. BA, DO-11-1, Nr. 8, ff. 72–4: HVDVP – Operativstab, 'Ergänzungsbericht zu den Vorkommnissen in Saalfeld', Berlin, 18 August 1951.

31. ThHStA, LBdVP, Bestand 5, Nr. 29, f. 7: Landesbehörde der Volkspolizei Thüringen, 'Aktennotiz über einen kurzen Bericht des Chefinspekteurs König an das Sekretariat der Landesleitung der Partei am 23.9.51', Weimar, 23 August 1951.

32. BA, DO-1-11, Nr. 8, ff. 81–2: HV Deutsche Volkspolizei (signed by Willi Seifert, Generalinspekteur der VP), Berlin, 31 August 1951.

33. BA, DO-1-11, Nr. 339, ff. 34–5: Der Chef der Deutschen Volkspolizei to the Generalsekretär der SED Walter Ulbricht, Berlin, 17 October 1951.

34. On the ABV-system, see Lindenberger, 'Die Deutsche Volkspolizei, pp. 115–17; Thomas Lindenberger, 'Der ABV im Text. Zur internen und öffentlichen Rede über die Deutsche Volkspolizei der 1950er Jahre', in Alf Lüdtke und Peter Becker (eds.), *Akten. Eingaben. Schaufenster. Die DDR und ihre Texte. Erkundungen zu Herrschaft und Alltag* (Berlin, 1997), pp. 136–66.

35. In December 1955 the Volkspolizei personnel numbered 99,376. See BA, DO-1-11, Nr. 1616, f. 95: 'Statistischer Bericht über den Zustand der Disziplin und der disziplaren Praxis für das Jahr 1955'. For statistics of the growth of the Volkspolizei (which give a slighltly different figure for 1955), see the tables in Lindenberger, 'Die Deutsche Volkspolizei', pp. 107, 132.

36. Richard Bessel, 'Policing, Professionalisation and Politics in Weimar Germany', in Clive Emsley and Barbara Weinberger (eds.), *Policing Western Europe. Politics, Professionalism, and Public Order, 1850–1940* (New York; Westport, Conn. and London), p. 190.

5

New York's Night of Birmingham Horror:
The NYPD, The Harlem Riot of 1964, and The Politics of "Law and Order"

Michael W. Flamm

The Occasion

In the afternoon of 16 July 1964, mere hours before Barry Goldwater accepted the Republican nomination and made 'crime in the streets' the issue at the forefront of his presidential campaign, an off-duty New York Police Department (NYPD) officer in plain clothes shot and killed a black teenager allegedly armed with a knife. The incident involved Lieutenant Thomas Gilligan, a seventeen-year veteran with a distinguished record, and James Powell, a fifteen-year-old summer-school student with a juvenile record. It occurred in Yorkville, a predominantly white section of Upper Manhattan, after the officer intervened in a dispute between a white superintendent and black teenagers congregated outside his building across the street from Robert Wagner Junior High School.[1]

Whether the shooting was justified remains unclear. Gilligan contended that it came after the youth had advanced on him in a menacing manner. But witnesses interviewed by reporters at the time and by the NAACP later contended that Powell (a slight youth) was unarmed and was moving away from Gilligan (a large man), who fired three times without warning or identification. In any event, the shooting triggered five nights of clashes between police and demonstrators in Harlem and Bedford-Stuyvesant (a black community in nearby Brooklyn). In the end, one person was killed, 141 were injured (including 48 officers), and 519 were arrested.[2]

The riot was hardly a new development for Harlem, the symbolic and historic heart of black America. In 1935 and 1943, police shootings had ignited large-scale civil disorders there. But in 1964 the NYPD committed a host of tactical errors. It neglected to take proper precautions in advance. It failed to exercise effective command control on the scene. And it raised the level of official force to dazzling and dangerous heights, serving notice that future riots would meet with equal if not greater firepower and fatalities. On the whole, the police response was confused and contradictory. In short, Harlem was not the 'finest hour' for New York's finest.

In the roll call of urban riots, commentators and scholars of the 1960s have tended to overlook Harlem. The Watts Riot of August 1965 caused greater shock, erupting amid the bungalows of Los Angeles less than two weeks after the signing of the Voting Rights Act. And the Detroit Riot of July 1967 featured greater bloodshed, forcing President Lyndon Johnson to deploy units of the 82nd and 101st Airborne to restore order. But it was the Harlem Riot which set the stage for a decade of racial unrest. A signal of what lay ahead, it also broadcast from the nation's media capital the powerful premiere of 'law and order,' an incendiary issue that would transform national politics in the coming years.

The Context

After World War II, racial tensions in New York reached new heights. Two decades of black migration helped change the complexion of the city – and the face of crime. During the 1950s, over 700,000 whites departed for the suburbs as more than 300,000 blacks arrived from the South. Disproportionately young and poor, the new arrivals contributed disproportionately, as both victim and perpetrator, to the rise in delinquency and disorder. 'They are afraid to say so in public,' reported *Time* in April 1958, 'but many of the North's big-city mayors groan in private that their biggest and most worrisome problem is the crime rate among Negroes.'[3]

The wave of crime created a wave of fear among whites which crested in July 1964. The statistics themselves were troubling. In the first six months of the year, murders rose 16.6 percent – rapes and robberies by 28 and 29 percent respectively. Subway crime jumped by almost 30 percent. But it was specific incidents that provoked alarm. On 21 April, a group of Jewish children were attacked by a gang of fifty black teenagers. On 10 May, the police confirmed the existence of the 'Blood Brothers', a black gang in Harlem believed responsible for the murder of four whites. And over Memorial Day weekend twenty black teens vandalised and terrorised a subway train, beating and robbing passengers at random. These events, warned the conservative *National Review*, represented more than just a deluge of delinquency: 'What is happening, or is about to happen – let us face it – is race war.'[4]

For their part, African Americans were upset over attacks on civil rights activists in the South, the racial overtones that the media was quick to affix to any incident of teenage violence, and years of perceived police brutality and neglect.[5] In early June, Whitney Young of the National Urban League (NUL) declared that crime was 'no stranger to Harlem. Its citizens have been victimised for years with amazing indifference on the part of the general public, which turned its eyes and thoughts elsewhere. The only new dimension to the current violence is that the frustrations of the ghetto are spilling out beyond its boundaries and directly affecting the public at large.'[6]

Crime was indeed no stranger to Harlem. The homicide and delinquency rates were, respectively, six and ten times the average for the rest of the city. Narcotics arrests were also disproportionately high. Social conditions added to the frustration. The unemployment rate for blacks was 25 percent, four times that of whites. The average black family in Harlem had an annual income well below that of the metropolitan area as a whole. The housing stock was in poor condition, but rents were higher than in comparable white neighbourhoods. And the schools were overcrowded and underfunded, with high dropout rates and low test scores.[7] The situation was ripe for a riot.

The Riot Itself

When it came, the NYPD's first blunder was a failure to take timely preventive measures. Of course, the absence of important civilian leaders was a contributing factor. Mayor Robert Wagner Jr. was travelling in Majorca and Congressman Adam Clayton Powell Jr. (no relation to James Powell) was in Switzerland, where he was vacationing and avoiding a libel claim won against him by an angry constituent. Governor Nelson Rockefeller was resting after the Republican Convention at a family property in Wyoming. Relaxing there as well was National Association for the Advancement of Colored People (NAACP) President Roy Wilkins. Their absence played an important if indeterminate role – as would Governor Edmund Brown's untimely trip to Greece shortly before the Watts Riot began.

Nevertheless, the NYPD had two days to prepare after the initial incident. The shooting of Powell occurred on a Thursday afternoon. That night and the following evening hundreds of teenagers protested over his death. Although the demonstrations were for the most part peaceful – one black officer was hurt when hit by a flying can of soda – they provided a clear indication of what was to come. Typically, the NYPD divided Harlem – the department's busiest jurisdiction – into three precincts and patrolled it with roughly 1,200 officers, about 85 percent of whom were white.[8] Yet the department chose not to commit additional personnel or declare a full alert until Sunday morning, causing many officers to arrive out of uniform and in piecemeal fashion. In addition, command posts and supply depots were not established and operational until Sunday evening. Nor were horse-mounted units committed in force until Tuesday night.[9] These delays would prove critical because the riot had actually begun in earnest on Saturday evening.

The riot started after a local minister urged a crowd of several hundred demonstrators, who had assembled to protest the disappearance of three civil rights workers in Mississippi, to march to the 28th Police Precinct and demand the arrest of Gilligan for murder. Police were able to clear the street in front of the station. But they were unable to control the crowd, which, joined by thousands of casual participants, rampaged throughout the fifty-seven square blocks of central Harlem. Despite the deployment of over 500 officers – including the entire Tactical Patrol Force, an elite unit of 300 officers, all under thirty years old, over six feet tall, and trained in judo – the NYPD could not establish a cordon around the area or contain the roving bands of rioters and looters.[10] With containment broken, chaos ensued along 125th Street, Harlem's commercial centre.[11]

The chaos was not inevitable, however. It was in large part a result of command control – or the lack thereof. In theory, the NYPD had detailed riot control plans updated as recently as 1958. In practice, officers – many of whom were in plain clothes, with only a badge pinned to their shirts or jackets as identification – were on their own once they reached Harlem. From headquarters, the general order was to control the crowds peacefully, using force only when necessary. From the street, the general sense was to use whatever tactics seemed to work. 'The idea is to make a lot of noise – run right at them yelling; that usually breaks up a crowd', said one sergeant, loosely interpreting the directive. When that failed, officers fired over the heads of the mobs and at the rooftops, where angry rioters were hurling bricks, bottles, and Molotov cocktails.'[12] Left without clear direction, the police were bewildered. 'Are we shooting *at* them?' an officer asked his partner. Command authority also broke down. 'I remember during the Harlem riots in 1964,' said one patrolman later,

> I saw guys down there shooting up at the rooftops trying to pin down people throwing bricks. ... And a lieutenant came along and said, 'Put that gun away. You have no authority to fire!' The cop told him, 'If you are afraid of getting hurt with gunfire around here, then get the hell out of here. I'm a cop sent up here to do a job and I am going to do a job.' At that point the lieutenant would ordinarily prefer charges against him. But this was a common thing in 1964; cops telling bosses 'don't try and stop me.'[13]

The description of the 'brass' as 'bosses' is suggestive. It exemplifies how, by the mid-1960s, a sense of police unionism had spread among the ranks.

The loss of command control contributed, amid the chaos and confusion, to a premature escalation of deadly force. By 3 a.m. Sunday morning officers had already fired at least 2,000 rounds and had run out of ammunition. In desperation, the department had boxloads of .38 calibre bullets shipped from the police pistol range in the Bronx and loaded onto a makeshift ordnance truck manned by two men armed with a shotgun and a machine gun. Like a scene from a classic western, the truck then raced through Harlem's darkened streets, delivering ammunition to embattled and grateful officers, many of whom were down to their final rounds.[14]

The use of gunfire – to which Commissioner Michael Murphy personally gave his approval at some point on Saturday evening (it is not clear precisely when) – was unprecedented for the NYPD. In both 1935 and 1943 it had ordered officers not to draw their weapons unless either they or civilians were in immediate danger. The response was also a violation of standard departmental procedure, which dictated first a show of force, then an order to disperse, followed by the use of night sticks, tear gas and – as a last resort only – firearms. The U.S. Army followed a similar doctrine.

'Volleys of "live" ammunition normally should not be fired over the heads of rioters,' advised riot expert Colonel Rex Applegate in his manual 'Kill or Get Killed'. In Detroit in 1967, General John Throckmorton followed regulations to the letter and permitted his paratroopers to load their weapons only if an officer on the scene gave the order. The soldiers soon restored peace to the streets with the expenditure of only 201 rounds, compared to the thousands expended by the NYPD in 1964.[15]

In Harlem, the show of firepower worked. The crowds dispersed and the loss of life was less than in 1943. Miraculously, only one rioter (an ex-convict) was killed and fifteen civilians were wounded, perhaps because of pure luck, perhaps because of 'superhuman restraint by cops with guns in their hands' according to a police captain.[16] 'We felt this means of control would be more effective and less harmful than the alternatives available to us,' said Deputy Commissioner Walter Arm, 'and we have been proven right.' But in a measure of departmental defensiveness, other spokesmen refused to say whether gunfire would become standard procedure (it did not) or explain why the NYPD had not employed tear gas, smoke grenades or horse-mounted patrols.[17]

Fundamentally, the resort to firearms was a risk of enormous, potentially tragic, proportions. Had the crowds become more assertive and less cowed, the NYPD would have had little alternative but to abandon its positions or aim its guns lower – and the bloodshed might have been unimaginable. Moreover, by scattering the crowds into small gangs, the police had rendered ineffective their tear gas and smoke grenades (which admittedly were already of little use against the rioters on the roofs). The NYPD had also complicated the task of controlling the looting and arson, which was usually the work of small bands of black residents. In the wake of the riot, Harlem business owners – African-American and Jewish-American – would complain bitterly about this failure. Why the department in 1964 had suffered the confusion that it had or chose the contradictory course of action that it did remains unclear. None of the top officials – in the NYPD or the Mayor's office – ever offered a clear, public explanation. The police archives are incomplete and inaccessible for the most part. The FBI investigation ordered by the White House concentrated on the root causes of the riot rather the police performance, although it took the NYPD to task for the shortage of black officers and the lack of riot training.[18] Therefore any explanation is almost by definition circumstantial rather than conclusive. Yet some possibilities merit mention.

One is that the NYPD was rife with internal conflict. At the top, there was constant turnover, with four commissioners in six years. Without strong leadership from One Police Plaza, the command structure wavered in the face of the crisis. At the bottom, there were ethnic and racial animosities between the overrepresented Irish and underrepresented blacks. 'Those were hellified times,' recalled a black officer. 'There was a clash of traditions which brought out animosities in all aspects.' Even after the minority hiring efforts of the late 1960s, African-Americans comprised less than 10 percent of all patrolmen – and only 4.7 percent of sergeants, 2.6 percent of lieutenants, and 1.4 percent of officers at or above the rank of captain. At the same time, the department remained 42 percent Irish. 'If it weren't for the Irish, there would be no police', observed former commissioner Francis Adams.[19]

In the middle, between the top brass and the rank-and-file, social and educational differences divided the commanders into two camps. The 'traditionalists' typically had little or no higher education and came from families with a history of service in the NYPD. They saw 'community relations' and 'riot containment' as forms of appeasement and surrender. The 'reformers' usually had attended college and had joined the department because of the security it offered during the Great Depression. Committed to police professionalism, they were now attaining positions of leadership.[20] In the aftermath of the riot, the tensions between these groups flourished.

At the same time, labour tensions between supervisors and patrolmen flourished. In the late 1950s, John Cassese rose to power within the Patrolmen's Benevolent Association (PBA) by challenging the mass transfer policies and anti-moonlighting initiatives of then-Commissioner Stephen Kennedy, who responded by dramatically shredding his PBA membership card during a televised press conference. During the early 1960s, Cassese consolidated his control of the union by demanding – and winning – improved pay and pension benefits for his membership. By 1964 police professionalism and police unionism coexisted uneasily. Now the NYPD operational structure faced an internal challenge from the newly empowered and politicised PBA, which emboldened individual officers to challenge their superiors.[21]

Another explanation, the subject of some media speculation at the time, was that the department was loathe to repeat what had happened in Birmingham, Alabama the year before, when Public Safety Commissioner Eugene 'Bull' Connor had unleashed tear gas, water cannons, and police dogs on black children marching against segregation. Ironically, the officers in Alabama and other southern states were reluctant to use their firearms for fear they would provoke the protesters. Yet news coverage in New York and around the world had nonetheless condemned their behaviour. It is therefore possible that the NYPD eschewed tear gas and other non-lethal measures because it did not wish to generate similar images or charges of brutality.[22] If so, the strategy proved remarkably unsuccessful as civil rights activists immediately and repeatedly employed the analogy. 'I saw New York's night of Birmingham horror', declared James Farmer of the Congress of Race Equality (CORE) the next day, and others echoed the theme.[23]

Aftermath

After the 'horror' had abated, the NYPD was unapologetic for the most part about its performance in the summer of 1964. The minimal loss of life alone, it contended, vindicated the actions taken. The department also conducted an internal investigation into the Gilligan shooting, but concluded that it was justified shortly after a grand jury found the officer not criminally liable for the shooting. Then in 1966 the PBA strenuously opposed a referendum, backed by black and white liberals, that would have permanently established a majority-civilian review board.

A PBA-sponsored television commercial surveyed the damage allegedly caused by the 1964 riot, with the commentator stating ominously that 'the police were so careful to avoid accusations that they were virtually powerless'.[24] A poll taken shortly before the election showed that a clear majority of those surveyed felt that the review board would hinder police performance. Ultimately, the compromise measure – many civil rights activists had wanted an all-civilian review board, which Mayor John Lindsay deemed too extreme – lost by a 2-1 margin in arguably the nation's most liberal city. Irish and Italian voters predictably opposed it in overwhelming numbers, but what particularly shocked many observers was that 55 percent of Jewish voters (especially the less affluent residents of the Bronx and Brooklyn) also opposed it even though supporters contended that it was a civil rights measure.[25]

In the meantime, however, the NYPD took measures to prevent a recurrence of the riot. In response to liberal complaints, it increased the number of black officers in Harlem. Ironically, the department had previously stationed relatively few black officers there because, in response to earlier demands by civil rights organisations, it had divided them equally among all precincts.[26] The NYPD also conceded (albeit implicitly and under the direction of a new commissioner) that the use of unrestricted gunfire was a mistake. In 1966 it adopted a new model of riot prevention. Subsequently known as the 'New York technique', it entailed a massive show of force and the formation of a perimeter, followed by a period of watching and waiting. When the situation cooled, officers gradually shortened the perimeter until the neighbourhood was back under control. Thanks in part to better tactics and training, New York would not suffer another major disorder for the rest of the decade.[27]

Other cities were less fortunate. As hundreds of riots erupted in 1967 and 1968, police departments would usually not resort to firearms on the scale or with the haste of the NYPD. But National Guard units would often emulate, consciously or not, the flawed 'New York model' of 1964. During the 'Long Hot Summer' of 1967, the tragic consequences were most vividly on display in Newark and Detroit, where many if not most of the deaths came at the hands of trigger-happy Guardsmen. Without the fire discipline of professional police officers, the overwhelmingly white 'weekend warriors' from suburban and small-town America proved singularly unsuited for riot control in minority-dominated urban areas.[28]

In the wake of those fiascos, the Kerner Commission in 1968 'nationalised' riot procedures. It recommended that departments engage in advanced training in non-lethal weaponry to avoid recourse to deadly force. It also urged the development of unit exercises to curb excessive individualism and mobilisation plans to limit unnecessary delays.[29] Had federal officials promoted such policies four years earlier, in the wake of Harlem, the disorders of the prior three years might have claimed fewer lives. But in the midst of the 1964 presidential campaign, with New York a critical battleground, the Johnson administration was reluctant to probe too deeply into the apparent 'success' of the NYPD.[30]

The Wider Reverberations

The political reverberations of Harlem were widespread and far-reaching, both at the time and in subsequent years. The riot divided liberals, who were uncertain whether the denial of civil liberties, economic opportunity or racial equality was the root cause.[31] But it united conservatives, who portrayed it as the logical outgrowth of civil disobedience run amok. Unable to attack the civil rights movement directly, they blamed it for the apparent rash of street crime, urban riots and political demonstrations, blending these distinct phenomena into a common threat to a society of decency, security and harmony – in short, to a society of 'law and order'.[32]

In New York, the riot exposed the city's racial fault lines for all to see. Ordinary whites generally saw Harlem as a race riot and saw themselves as the clear target of the mobs. A woman living on Morningside Heights reported that the 125th Street Subway Station featured a large sign reading 'Kill All Whites'. She declared that she could not go to work without fear of robbery or death.[33] By contrast, black leaders typically identified police brutality as the precipitating factor. 'I saw a blood bath. I saw with my own eyes violence, a bloody orgy of police [violence]', charged Farmer, supported by Congressman Powell and the *Amsterdam News*. 'This was a war – a war between the citizens of Harlem and the police.'[34] Even the moderate NAACP sharply criticised the NYPD for employing 'excessive force' in confronting the demonstrators and stated categorically that the riot 'was anti-police'.[35]

In Washington, the riot generated shock and surprise. In public, President Johnson kept his composure, pledging to restore order, promising to attack the social conditions which fostered the riot, and directing FBI Director J. Edgar Hoover to investigate its causes.[36] In private, anxiety pervaded the White House. 'It is by now clear that civil disorder will be the central domestic issue of the election', warned one aide. 'Every Negro riot represents tens of thousands of Goldwater votes.' A memo to the President on the eve of a campaign swing through New York warned that addressing the riot issue directly might benefit Goldwater, but it also might 'blunt the further erosion of white voter passions' – a critical concern given the possibility of future riots. 'This one issue could destroy us in the campaign', concluded the memo. 'Therefore we need to move swiftly to try to hold the line before it spreads like a contagion.'[37]

Johnson himself was deeply troubled. 'Everybody thinks ... if we denounce the killings in Mississippi [the murder of three civil rights workers] ... we ought to denounce it in Harlem too,' he told an aide on July 20 (Monday evening). 'And we haven't done a damn thing about it.' The next day the President called Hoover. 'We're getting floods of wires and telegrams', Johnson told him. 'Here's one. [reads aloud:] "I'm a working girl. ... I'm afraid to leave my house. ... I feel the Negro revolution will reach Queens. ... Please send troops immediately to Harlem."' The President chose instead to send the FBI director to investigate the riot, informing him that 'I think the Communists are in charge of it.' In subsequent conversations with New York Mayor Robert Wagner and Texas Governor John Connally, Johnson also speculated that right-wing extremists like Texas oil millionaire H.L. Hunt were involved. 'Both sides are in on these riots,' he told Connally. 'Hell, these folks have got walkie-talkies. ... Somebody's financing them big. ... It's Brooklyn one night and it's Harlem the next night and it'll be another section of New York tonight.'[38]

In September, Hoover released the FBI's findings on 'Recent Civil Disturbances in Urban Areas', which allayed some – but certainly not all – of Johnson's anxiety. It stated that 'there was no systematic planning or organisation of any of the city riots', not by radical individuals, the Communist Party or conservative zealots. The report also refused to characterise the disorders as race riots or contend that they were the direct result of civil rights agitation. Instead, it stressed the impact of slum conditions and the need for riot control to remain a local matter – federalism in practice as well as theory.[39] The report's moderate tone won praise from liberals and scorn from conservatives. The *National Review* expressed outrage at the explicit 'politicisation' of the FBI and the implicit 'endorsement' of the anti-poverty program.[40]

In October, Johnson made a fateful decision in large part because of the political fallout from the Harlem Riot. Seeking to protect his right flank from charges that he was 'soft' on 'law and order', he uttered the words that would haunt his administration and liberalism in the years to come. 'The war on poverty,' he declared, 'is a war against crime and a war against disorder.'[41] By bonding the 'War on Poverty' to a 'War on Crime', the President had garnered political support and expressed the liberal belief that it was vital to attack the 'root causes' of crime – but he had also doubled the scope of each 'war' as well as its exposure to a withering conservative counterfire. By accepting the coupling of crime and riots, he had moreover complicated any serious attempt to reform police practices or separate the real from the imagined racial fears of white urbanites and suburbanites. The next four years would see the administration consumed by the fight against street crime and civil disorder. By 1968 Richard Nixon was able, using dubious but persuasive logic, to cite the simultaneous rise in street crime and social spending as proof that both domestic wars were costly failures – and to assert without irony that the first civil right of all Americans was freedom from violence.[42] In the debate over law and order, conservatives had thus inverted the arguments and appropriated the language of liberals. In the process, the right had reshaped national politics. It had transformed the personal security crisis of the 1960s into the equivalent of the national security scare of the 1950s.[43]

Ironically, Harlem had seemed in 1964 like a distant place and problem to most officials within the Johnson administration, who had contempt for the standards of southern law enforcement but respected the professionalism of northern police departments. 'We just thought they've got a big fine police department and they can take care of it', recalled Attorney General Ramsay Clark.[44] In retrospect, that attitude – so pregnant of federalism and so prevalent when Watts erupted a year later – was a major reason why liberals faced a crisis of credibility by 1968.[45]

Notes

1. From the window of a TV repair shop, Gilligan saw an argument erupt over whether the superintendent had intentionally or accidentally sprayed the teens with water. Powell got a knife and chased the superintendent into the building. After failing to catch him, Powell encountered Gilligan, threatened the officer with a knife, and was shot dead. See James Lardner, *Crusader: The Hell-Raising Police Career of Detective David Durk* (New York, 1996), p. 75. Yorkville was a German neighbourhood that supposedly had harboured pro-Nazi sentiments at one point. Two years later, during the Civilian Review Board controversy, Mayor John Lindsay charged that a neo-Nazi group regularly distributed literature there. See Ruth Cowan, 'The New York City Civilian Review Board Referendum of November 1966', Ph.D. dissertation (New York University, 1970), pp. 346–347.
2. 'Statement and Recommendations of New York Branch NAACP Regarding July Social Unrests in Harlem Area,' NY Branch – 1964–65, Box C103, Group III, NAACP Papers, Manuscript Division, Library of Congress [hereafter NAACP Papers, LOC]; 'Harlem: Hatred in the Streets', *Newsweek*, 3 August 1964, p. 19. Property losses ranged into the hundreds of thousands of dollars.
3. Gerald Sorin, *The Nurturing Neighbourhood: The Brownsville Boys Club and Jewish Community in Urban America, 1940–1990* (New York, 1990), p. 158. 'The Negro Crime Rate: A Failure in Integration', *Time*, 21 April 1958, p.16. A similar account appeared in *U.S. News* in December. 'There is a big, untold story in the big cities of this country. The story keeps growing rapidly – unnoted in the news of the day'. After citing arrest and crime records from Philadelphia, the article observed that blacks were now the largest single voting bloc in the city, controlling 14 of 58 wards and enabling the Democrats to end 67 years of Republican supremacy. 'The Big Story in the Big Cities', *U.S. News & World Report* 45, 19 December 1958, pp. 46–54.
4. 'Rise in Murders Reported by City', *The New York Times*, 18 July 1964, p. 23; 'Gangs Beat and Rob 2 Riders on Upper Manhattan Subways', *The New York Times*, 18 July 1964, p. 23; 'Maccabees and the Mau Mau', *National Review*, 16 July 1964, pp. 479–480.

5. As James Baldwin wrote, 'the only way to police a ghetto is to be oppressive. None of the police commissioner's men, even with the best will in the world, have any way of understanding the lives led by the people they swagger about in twos and threes controlling. Their very presence is an insult, and it would be, even if they spent their entire day feeding gumdrops to children. They represent the force of the white world, and that world's criminal profit and ease, to keep the black man corraled up here, in his place. The badge, the gun in the holster, and the swinging club make vivid what will happen should his rebellion become overt.' Policemen are hated in the ghetto – and are often shocked and dismayed by the fact: 'There is no way for him not to know it: there are few things under heaven more unnerving than the silent, accumulating contempt and hatred of a people. He moves through Harlem, therefore, like an occupying soldier in a bitterly hostile country; which is precisely what, and where he is, and is the reason he walks in twos and threes.' James Baldwin, *Nobody Knows My Name* (New York, 1962), pp. 65–67.

6. 'There has always been crime and rioting,' he observed, presciently, 'particularly among the poor of all races and nations, and especially wherever full citizenship, liberty, and opportunity were denied.' Among the solutions the NUL advocated were jobs programs, public works projects, better schools, improved housing, and an end to the use of racial identities in crime stories. See Press Conference, 4 June 1964, 'News Media on the Manifestation of Teenage Violence', Box 43, Part 2, National Urban League Papers, Manuscript Division, Library of Congress [hereafter NUL Papers, LOC].

7 In 1963, 29.2 percent of black men were unemployed at some point during the year – a majority were out of work fifteen weeks or more. See Daniel Patrick Moynihan, *The Negro Family: The Case for National Action* (Washington DC: Dept. of Labour, 1965), p. 4; and 'Harlem: Hatred in the Streets', *Newsweek*, 3 August 1964, pp. 19–20. In New York underemployment averaged 30 percent in Harlem and Bedford-Stuyvesant, and between 1963 and 1965 there were no gains in manufacturing employment, despite annual growth nationally of 7 percent. By 1966 the unemployment rate in urban black slums was almost three times the national average (9.3 percent to 3.5 percent). See Richard A. Cloward and Frances Fox Piven, *Regulating the Poor: The Functions of Public Welfare* (New York, 1971), pp. 216–217.

8. Overall, the NYPD had 25,000 officers, making it the nation's largest force. Drug traffic made Harlem the department's busiest jurisdiction. 'No Place Like Home', *Time*, 31 July 1964, p. 16.

9. 'New York City Deep in Trouble', *U.S. News & World Report*, 3 August 1964, p. 22.

10. The TPD was formed in 1958 in the wake of news reports suggesting that the black migration had contributed to a dramatic surge in lawlessness. 'They are afraid to say so in public,' reported *Time* in April 1958, 'but many of the North's big-city mayors groan in private that their biggest and most worrisome problem is the crime rate among Negroes.' For crimes involving violence or the threat of bodily harm – murder, manslaughter, rape, robbery, and aggravated assault – arrest figures from New York, Chicago, and Detroit indicated that black males were overwhelmingly overrepresented. See 'The Negro Crime Rate: A Failure in Integration', *Time*, 21 April 1958, p.16. See also 'The Big Story in the Big Cities', *U.S. News & World Report*, 19 December 1958, p. 46–54.

11. Paul L. Montgomery and Francis X. Clines, 'Thousands Riot in Harlem Area; Scores Are Hurt', *The New York Times*, 19 July 1964, pp. 1, 54. The NYPD

mobilized all 25,000 officers and put them on 12-hour shifts. Operations were directed by Chief Inspector Lawrence J. McKearney, who was stationed at the 28th Precinct. R.W. Apple Jr, 'Violence Flares Again in Harlem; Restraint Urged', *The New York Times*, 20 July 1964, pp. 1, 16; and 'Harlem: Hatred in the Streets', *Newsweek*, 3 August 1964, p. 16.

12. Baseball star Jackie Robinson helped to defuse the potential riot, which nonetheless persuaded the NYPD to revise procedures which in most instances dated back to the late 1930s. Francis X. Clines, 'Policemen Exhaust Their Ammunition in All-Night Battle', *The New York Times*, 20 July 1964, p. 1.

13. Nicholas Alex, *New York Cops Talk Back: A Study of a Beleagured Minority* (New York, 1976), p.75.

14. Francis X. Clines, 'Policemen Exhaust Their Ammunition in All-Night Battle', *The New York Times*, 20 July 1964, p. 1.

15. R.W. Apple Jr., 'Police Defend the Use of Gunfire in Controlling Riots in Harlem', *The New York Times*, 21 July 1964, pp. 1, 22. Throckmorton attempted to have the National Guard unload their weapons as well, but had less success. *Report of the National Advisory Commission on Civil Disorders* (New York, 1968), p. 100. See also 'An American Tragedy, 1967', *Newsweek*, 7 August 1967, p. 20.

16. Apparently, the bullets fell harmlessly to the ground once the muzzle velocity was spent. 'New York City Deep in Trouble', *U.S. News & World Report*, 3 August 1964, p. 22.

17. R.W. Apple Jr., 'Police Defend the Use of Gunfire'.

18. The report also criticised civilian review boards for handcuffing the ability of police departments to respond – a finding that reinforced the PBA brief two years later. *FBI Report*, 18 September 1964 (released on 26 September 1964), 'Justice Department', Office Files of Richard Goodwin, Box 20, Lyndon Baines Johnson Presidential Library, University of Texas, Austin, Texas (hereafter LBJ Library).

19. See Leonard Ruchelman, *Police Politics: A Comparative Study of Three Cities* (Cambridge, Mass., 1974), p. 13; and 'Blacks Remain Underrepresented in NYPD', *The New York Times*, 12 February 1973, p. 1. See also Lawrence M. Friedman, *Crime and Punishment in American History* (New York: Basic Books, 1993), p. 377; Stephen Leinen, *Black Police, White Society* (New York, 1984), p. 99; and Arthur Niederhoffer, *Behind the Shield: The Police in Urban Society* (New York, 1967), pp. 16, 36, 133, 135.

20. During the depression, a top-grade patrolman earned $3000 and had job security. Consequently, many college graduates joined the force. Of the 300 recruits who joined the NYPD in June 1940, more than 50 percent had college degrees. These men now formed the core of the elite group promoting professionalism. By contrast, postwar prosperity meant that over the past fifteen years 95 percent of NYPD candidates had no college training. Thus one police scholar saw an internal revolution between the reformers in favour of professionalism and the traditionalists who opposed it, although he also acknowledged that both sides had ample incentives to compromise. 'The traditionalists liked the idea of higher salaries, greater prestige and autonomy. The professionals had to demonstrate that they were cops first and not bow to minority pressure. ... And of course they sought to get ahead – and many were socialized by the force itself.' Niederhoffer, *Behind the Shield*, pp. 3–4, 16, 36.

21. See Thomas R. Brooks, '"No!" Says the P.B.A.', *The New York Times Magazine*, 16 October 1966; and Ruchelman, *Police Politics: A Comparative Study of Three Cities*, pp. 81–85.

22. R.W. Apple Jr., 'Police Defend the Use of Gunfire'.
23. 'When Night Falls', *Time*, 31 July 1964, pp. 10, 16.
24. Bernard Weinraub, 'Kennedy Sees Peril to Civilian Control of Police', *The New York Times*, 4 November 1966, p. 29.
25. For a complete description of this important moment, see Michael W. Flamm, "'Law and Order': Street Crime, Civil Disorder, and the Crisis of Liberalism', Ph.D. dissertation (Columbia University, 1998), chapter four.
26. After the riot, five black sergeants replaced five white officers in Harlem precincts, again in response to calls from civil rights activists. Gershon Jacobson, 'Black and White', *The New Republic*, 8 August 1964, p. 15. 'When Night Falls', *Time*, 31 July 1964.
27. Lardner, *Crusader: The Hell-Raising Police Career of Detective David Durk*, p. 83.
28. For example, only 1.2 percent of the New Jersey National Guard was black. *Report of the National Advisory Commission on Civil Disorders*, p. 67.
29. The commission also recommended improved operational planning, particularly in areas like command and control and communications. And it advised equipping the police with improved protective gear such as gas masks. However, it opposed providing advanced weaponry. 'We should not attempt to to convert our police into combat troops equipped for urban warfare', the commission concluded. *Report of the National Advisory Commission on Civil Disorders*, 'Supplement on Control of Disorder', pp. 484–493.
30. After the riots in Harlem and Rochester, Johnson made an impassioned request to his FBI liaison: 'Deke, you and the FBI have got to stop these riots. One of my political analysts tells me that every time one occurs, it costs me 90,000 votes.' Cartha 'Deke' DeLoach, *Hoover's FBI: The Inside Story by Hoover's Trusted* (Washington, DC, 1995), p. 279.
31. Theodore White, *The Making of the President 1964* (New York, 1965), p. 231.
32. See Michael W. Flamm, "'Law and Order'", chapter two.
33. Rockefeller's correspondence contained an overwhelming number of similar letters. 'The situation in New York City is getting out of hand', wrote a LaSalle Street resident who, like most whites, also drew no distinction between street crime and civil disorder. 'Violence, horror, looting, rioting, stabbing, raping, purse-snatching are all around. ... It is not safe walking in the streets and parks and riding in the elevators.' Letter, Mrs. Gertrude Schwebell of 549 Riverside Drive to Rockefeller, 19 July 1964, Reel 17, RG 15, Gubernatorial Office Records, Subject Files, Nelson A. Rockefeller Collection, Rockefeller Archives Centre, Tarrytown, NY (hereafter NAR Collection, RAC); letter, Mr. Charles Shamoon of 70 La Salle St. to Rockefeller, 24 July 1964, Reel 17, RG 15, Gubernatorial Office Records, Subject Files, NAR Collection, RAC.
34. 'Harlem: Hatred in the Streets', *Newsweek*, 3 August 1964, p. 17. '"The black man is mad," declared Powell, "mad with the continued police brutality of white policemen."' Woody Klein, 'Harlem: The Ghetto Ignites', *The Nation*, 10 August 1964, pp. 50–51.
35. 'Statement and Recommendations of New York Branch NAACP Regarding July Social Unrests in Harlem Area', p. 4, NY Branch – 1964–65, Box C103, Group III, NAACP Papers, LOC.
36. Johnson also carefully paired his criticism of the riots in the North with condemnation of white supremacist violence in the South. 'American citizens', he said, 'have a right to protection of life and limb – whether driving along a highway in Georgia, a road in Mississippi, or a street in New York City.' Although he called the

need for order 'the immediate overriding issue', he added that 'there can be no compromise in securing equal and exact justice for all Americans'. Statement on Investigation by the FBI of Recent Civil Disturbances in New York City, 21 August 1964, 'Report of the U.S. Senate Committee on Commerce', Box 16, 1964 Campaign Files, Goldwater Papers, Arizona Historical Foundation, Tempe, Arizona.

37. Memo, Adam Walinsky, n.d., attached to memo, Adam Yarmolinsky to Douglass Cater, 10 August 1964, 'Misc. Correspondence, 1964', Office Files of S. Douglass Cater, Box 17, LBJ Library; unsigned memo, Office of Jack Valenti to Johnson, 27 July 1964, Ex JL 3, WHCF, Box 25, LBJ Library. The memo may have been written by Adam Walinsky, who made a strikingly similar statement in a memo to Douglass Cater on 10 August 1964.

38. Michael R. Beschloss, *Taking Charge: The Johnson White House Tapes, 1963–1964* (New York, 1997), pp. 459, 462, 466–467.

39. *FBI Report*, 18 September 1964 (released on 26 September 1964), 'Justice Department', Office Files of Richard Goodwin, Box 20, LBJ Library.

40. 'Bulletin', *National Review*, 13 October 1964, p. 1. Ironically, the FBI director had hopes and designs of his own. In July, shortly after an uneasy peace had returned to Harlem, he met with the President, who wanted an investigation that would contain the political fallout from the riots and shield his "Great Society" from conservative criticism. Johnson had already recruited former presidential candidate Thomas Dewey as a ghostwriter for the FBI report, hoping that he would restrain Hoover. Instead, the roles were reversed, with the director currying White House favour by moderating Dewey's analysis. In the end, the report benefited both the President and Hoover. Johnson, as one historian has noted, had 'covertly maneuvered a prominent Republican and overtly maneuvered his anticommunist FBI director into issuing a report that endorsed the War on Poverty and helped blunt the Goldwater Republican challenge'. In exchange for his moderation, Hoover had gained a freer hand with surveillance operations. The tacit bargain would have significant consequences in the years to come. In particular, it would lead to expanded surveillance of black radicals during the Johnson administration – and to COINTELPRO operations during the Nixon administration. See Kenneth O'Reilly, 'The FBI and the Politics of the Riots, 1964–1968', *Journal of American History* 75 (June 1988), pp. 94–98. See also Kenneth O'Reilly, *'Racial Matters': The FBI's Secret File on Black America, 1960–1972* (New York, 1989), pp. 233–236.

41. Speech, Dayton, OH, 16 October 1964, 'Report of the U.S. Senate Committee on Commerce', Box 16, 1964 Campaign Files, Goldwater Papers, AHF.

42. 'Let us recognize that the first civil right of every American is to be free from domestic violence', declared Richard Nixon at the Republican National Convention. Of the 'silent majority' he added: 'They are not racists or sick; they are not guilty of the crime that plagues the land.' He further noted that 'a nation that can't keep the peace at home won't be trusted to keep the peace abroad'. Although the 'War on Poverty' has led to 'an ugly harvest of frustration, violence and failure across the land', he promised that 'the wave of crime is not going to be the wave of the future in America. ... To those who say law and order is the code word for racism, this is our reply: Our goal is justice for every American.' Presidential Nomination Acceptance Speech, 8 August 1968, PPS 208 (1968) 58.11.2, Speech Files, Nixon Presidential Library, Yorba Linda, California.

43. Contemporary observers often noted this analogy. See for example James Q. Wilson, 'Crime in the Streets', *The Public Interest* 5 (Fall 1966), pp. 26–35,

reprinted in Marvin R. Summers and Thomas E. Barth (eds.) *Law and Order in a Democratic Society* (Columbus, Ohio, 1970), pp. 14–15.

44. 'We were so consumed with the South and there was so much to be done there and so little that we had the potential to do, [that] when we thought of the North we didn't think of civil rights then really. … It was August 11, 1965, before we – and that was the beginning of Watts – really focused on the problem of the riots in the big cities.' Transcript, Ramsey Clark Oral History Interview, 11 February 1969, by Harri Baker, p. 22, LBJ Library.

45. 'We just simply hadn't seen the warnings', conceded then Deputy Attorney General Ramsey Clark. Transcript, Ramsey Clark Oral History Interview, 21 March 1969, by Harri Baker, pp. 4 and 6, LBJ Library. 'The President, and all of us, were baffled by it for a long time', recalled aide Harry McPherson. 'Our data was almost nonexistent. It took us several days to understand that Watts was not a conventional eastern city tenement area, but it was an area of small houses.' Transcript, Harry McPherson Oral History Interview, 9 April 1969, by T.H. Baker, tape #7, p. 1, LBJ Library.

6

Policing Pit Closures, 1984–1992

David Waddington and Chas Critcher

On a hot June day in 1984, at the height of the year-long national miners' strike in opposition to pit closures, 10,000 miners, their wives, families and supporters, marched from Kings Cross railway station to a lobby of parliament. After minor incidents en route, seventy people were arrested during disturbances in Parliament. One eye witness identified the heavy-handed arrest of a demonstrator as the turning point:

> He was thrown headlong over a crash barrier, pounced on by seven policemen and then dragged through traffic by a police van. As uproar broke out, the familiar sight of two dozen police on horses forced the lobbyers and the public onto either side of the road. Arrests were many as police horses crushed miners against the walls and railings of parliament, forcing them to spill forward onto the road where snatch squads arrested them.[1]

Lloyd argues that access to the lobby was 'over-policed and restricted' and police intervention was unnecessarily punitive, especially towards female demonstrators.[2]

Eight years later, in October 1992, in a renewed campaign against pit closures, 50,000 miners and their sympathisers again marched through London. But there was no disorder. 'Although there were a few anxious moments, the day's protest was concluded peacefully and without any arrests. There was an exchange of mutual thanks between the National Union of Mineworkers (NUM) and the Metropolitan Police.'[3] That two such similar events should have such different outcomes is but one example from our lengthy research programme into why some political protests produce disorder while others do not.

In 1984, we were about to embark on an ESRC-funded study of public order in South Yorkshire when the year long miners' strike began. It provided us with an extended case study for the central question which initially guided the research: is it possible to identify the factors which can explain whether and to what extent public disorder occurs in the political arena? In endeavouring to answer this, we developed the 'flashpoints model' of public disorder, which identifies such factors at six interrelated levels of analysis.[4] During and after the strike, there emerged a debate about the efficacy and desirability of what was termed paramilitary policing. We therefore formulated an additional focus of enquiry: how far does paramilitary policing as a concept capture the changing nature of police strategy and what evidence is there for its effectiveness in averting public disorder?

We begin our discussion by reviewing the police role within the miners' strike. We then outline the development of the flashpoints model, initially from two rallies which occurred in Sheffield, early in the stoppage; and subsequently from the 'notorious' case of the Orgreave picket. To exemplify how any model should be able to explain order as well as disorder, we then analyse the peaceful 1992 London demonstration. The long-standing debate about paramilitary policing is assessed in the light of our research findings. Finally, we offer some recommendations about which police strategies would contribute to the maintenance of public order – surely one of the key objectives of policing in a democratic society.

Delegitimation and Disorder:
The 1984–5 Miners' Strike

The national miners' strike of 1984–5 arose from opposition by the NUM to the economic and social effects of a secret programme for pit closures. Following the sudden closure of the Cortonwood colliery in South Yorkshire, the NUM authorised strike action by miners in the union's most militant areas. This action, constitutional under NUM rules, obviated the need for a national ballot, disempowering those who might have voted against industrial action. The NUM's strategy was to picket working mines. The year-long strike was eventually defeated, due not least to the police's ability to ensure that working miners could continue entering pits and to enable strike-breakers to return to work.[5]

Memoirs of Conservative cabinet ministers confirm that the Government's entire strike strategy reflected years of contingency planning for a showdown with the miners.[6] It was intended both to exact revenge on the NUM for two strike defeats in the 1970s (which contributed to the loss of a General Election), and permanently to nullify the political threat posed by the NUM and its leadership[7]. The Prime Minister's own memoirs emphasise how: 'It was crucial for the future of the industry and for the future of the country itself that the NUM's claim that uneconomic pits should never be closed should be defeated, and be seen to be defeated, and the use of strikes for political purposes discredited once and for all.'[8] Control of the police was effectively assumed by the Home Secretary in regular secret briefing sessions with Chief Constables. Two weeks into the strike he made his views public:

> The legal position is clear. Any attempt to obstruct or intimidate those who wish to go to work is a breach of the criminal law. The mere presence of large numbers of pickets can be intimidating. The police have a duty to prevent obstruction and intimidation and enable those who wish to go to work to do so. They have the power to stop and disperse large numbers of pickets and to take preventive action by stopping vehicles and people.[9]

Clear signals were sent to the police about the actions which were expected of them. These were converted into a range of tactics largely unprecedented, at least in post-war Britain. The five key features were:

1) systematic national co-ordination of the normally localised police forces

To thwart the NUM's picketing strategy, the police deployed 20,000 riot police, centrally coordinated by the National Reporting Centre inside Scotland Yard.[10] The massive police operation began in the first few days of the strike. 8,000 police officers were despatched to head off pickets in Derbyshire and Nottinghamshire. 'This initial high-profile policing, before any major confrontation had taken place, did much to set the tone for the dispute.'[11]

2) use of roadblocks to turn back pickets

Cars and coaches carrying pickets were turned back by police on the spurious grounds that they were 'likely to cause a breach of the peace'. Those evading roadblocks were kept well away from working miners, whose buses were allowed through at high speed, in clear breach of the convention that pickets should be allowed to speak to those continuing to work.[12]

3) arbitrary arrests

Even apparently innocuous offences, like shouting 'scab', frequently resulted in arrests.[13] Miners, their wives and sympathisers were verbally abused, taunted by the waving of police pay packets (symbolic of their huge overtime payments) and provoked by the rhythmic drumming of batons on riot shields.

4) provocative police presence and equipment

Sheffield Police Watch noted:

> that in the majority of cases where violence breaks out this is due to police tactics and when there is what we describe as over-policing. We have repeatedly noticed that when the police arrive at a peaceful picket in overwhelming numbers and with dogs, horses, riot equipment and ambulances, then the atmosphere changes. Time and again we have seen this equipment deployed with little or no justification. In our view, it is inevitable that some pickets will retaliate when arrested arbitrarily and for no reason attacked by police dogs. [14]

5) severe bail conditions

Magistrates imposed exceptional bail conditions on those arrested, in order to curtail picketing.[15]

Maintaining order had here come to mean following instructions from government to break the strike. The police may have undertaken this role only under extreme pressure.[16] including a threat to use the army.[17] Nevertheless, senior officers publicly allied themselves with working as against striking miners[18]. McCabe and Wallington conclude that 'the police gave systematic priority to achieving the objectives of one party to an industrial dispute, to the detriment of normal police services, through a mistaken assessment of their priorities or in response to pressure, or both'.[19]

This view has been endorsed by others:

> The police were guilty of collaborating with the government. Senior policemen could have publicised the possibility of using civil remedies

and in the final analysis they could have refused to do the government's dirty work for them. The police did the bidding of the government and the Coal Board, but the police are there to administer the common good not just to do the government's will.[20]

In this highly charged atmosphere, where the police seemed to have forsaken any pretence of acting within a legally defined and publicly accountable framework, the policing of public order proceeded. It is our contention, and will be central to our model and discussion, that this overarching political context defined the parameters of policing. Since this was known by both police *and* policed to be their assumed role, it was difficult to maintain the ideal or illusion that the police were neutral guardians of public order.

Case Studies 1 and 2: The NUM Rallies in Sheffield, April 1984

In this section, we briefly recount two case studies which informed much of our early thinking about the policing of public disorder, if only because they involved two apparently identical scenarios which produced quite different outcomes.

The first rally took place outside the NUM headquarters in St James's Square, Sheffield. Police estimated that it involved 7,000 miners and their supporters from across the UK, and 2,000 police officers from ten separate constabularies.[21] Striking miners sought to persuade their national executive to reject a motion calling for a nationwide ballot. The police operation was designed to protect from harassment representatives of both pro-strike areas (Yorkshire, Scotland and South Wales) and anti-strike areas (Nottinghamshire and Leicestershire).

The arrival of executive members opposed to the strike precipitated a series of violent confrontations. Miners linked arms and drove into the ranks of police officers, standing ten deep thirty yards from the main building. Further confrontation followed when the NUM's national president, Arthur Scargill, appeared at an upper-storey window to denounce the both the police presence and the ongoing 'butchery' of the coal industry. Each time the police not only withstood the charges but, chanting 'One two! One, two!' pushed the demonstrators to the rear of the courtyard. Punching, kicking and hair-pulling were commonplace.

After the meeting, the NUM president emerged to inform his members that the motion for a strike ballot had been ruled 'out of order' and would now be referred to a Special Delegates' Conference in seven days' time, which would also consider amending the union rules so that a simple majority, rather than the 55 percent currently stipulated, would constitute a sufficient mandate for a strike. Amidst the euphoria that followed, miners launched a final defiant surge into the police lines.

The contrast in mood and conduct between this and the second rally, exactly one week later, was remarkable. On the second occasion, a carnival atmosphere prevailed across an entirely peaceful affair in which no arrests were made. The same parties were involved, with apparently the same sentiments being expressed, yet measures had been taken to avert disorder.

The negative publicity after the previous week's rally predisposed both the NUM and the police to conciliation. Sheffield City Council and the South Yorkshire Police Committee liaised between the two sides, producing a common plan. The police agreed to a low-key strategy, the NUM to appoint stewards. A more manageable venue, the City Hall, was nominated. A platform was erected to occupy the crowd with speakers and entertainers. Two Nottinghamshire delegates, who had sided with the national union against the views of their local members, were personally accompanied into the hall by the leader of the NUM. The second rally showed how 'even the most conflict-ridden situation can be kept orderly, given accommodation between the two parties involved'.[22]

The Flashpoints Model of Disorder

Our analysis of these two rallies and other demonstrations, pickets and community disorders occurring in South Yorkshire prior to the strike revealed a number of factors crucial to an orderly or disorderly outcome. For the rallies, the key differences included the following:

- the degree of formal consultation and agreement between the police and the demonstrating group
- the consequent agreements about the venue and its layout (the management of space)
- the specific provision for the crowd's sentiments to find formal and conventional expression, rather than being improvised and hence volatile

- the ways in which symbolic persons and moments were exploited by key personnel to invite orderly or disorderly responses
- the ways in which potential flashpoints were sparked or defused by the actions of the organisers and the police

Composing lists of factors of this kind eventually led us to construct a model of the processes involved at all levels, from the widest political context to the face to face interactions during the event itself. This was the flashpoints model, which over the last ten years we have explained in detail and applied to a wide range of public order situations, including the urban disturbances of the early 1980s, the anti-poll tax riot in London in 1990 and animal export protests during 1995.[23] A brief summary will suffice here.

The objective of the flashpoints model is to incorporate relevant variables into a general framework for explaining different types of disorder. Its principal achievement is in highlighting the conjunction of circumstances. 'It is not the presence or absence of an individual element which is important so much as how elements fuse and interact.'[24] The model incorporates six interdependent levels of analysis: structural, political/ideological, cultural, contextual, situational and interactional.

The *structural* level refers to macro-sociological factors – notably, material inequalities, political impotence and inferior life-chances – which form the bases of subjective deprivation and resentment in society. Latent social conflict is more likely to become manifest when the state fails to respond to an expressed grievance, since this leads protestors to feel that they have no stake in the moral order.

The next level of our model, the *political/ideological*, encompasses how key political and ideological institutions (e.g. political parties, the police, the media and opinion leaders) react to dissenting groups. The legitimacy accorded to the groups' declared ends and means is fundamental. Vilification will simultaneously alienate them and invite police repression.

The *cultural* level concerns the ways of life and thought that groups develop on the basis of shared experiences, including definitions of 'us' and 'them'. What appears crucial is the construction of a consensus between police and protestors about the behavioural norms appropriate to the situation. Its absence prefigures disorder.

The *contextual* level focuses on the dynamic communication processes which help to determine the emotive significance of an encounter. A negative history of interaction between the police and dissenting group may sensitise the situation. The potential for disorder can be amplified by rumour, media sensationalism, or threatening statements by police or protest leaders. Conversely, some degree of trust between the parties may be established, at least for the duration of the event, through liaison between representatives.

The *situational* level refers to spatial or social determinants of order or disorder. Features of any particular location, such as the extent to which it facilitates police surveillance of the crowd or prevents demonstrators feeling trapped, will enhance the prospects of order. Space also has a symbolic meaning: a group may feel they have a right to be there, the police that such a right is conditional upon the rights of others to pass freely. The appearance of 'targets of derision' (such as members of a rival political faction) may trigger disorder, especially if the police have to intervene. The way that space is managed by both parties is another vital consideration. Wherever demonstrations are self-policed, when the organisers are at pains to disavow violence, there are points of interest (e.g., speakers and entertainers) to capture the crowd's interest, and symbolic mechanisms for expressing dissent (e.g., a minute's silence), disorder is more likely to be averted. Alternatively, a heavy police presence in riot gear or the use of horses and dogs may prove provocative.

The *interactional* level deals with the quality of relations on the ground between police and protestors. These will vary in degrees of respect, cooperation, restraint or provocation. In highly charged situations, a particular incident (the throwing of a brick, an arrest or police charge) may spark off disorder. Such 'flashpoints' are interpreted symbolically as indicating the underlying attitude of the other side. Important are intensifiers – i.e., characteristics of the individuals involved (whether high-ranking or from a 'vulnerable' category, such as a woman, old person or child), or the way in which they are perpetrated (e.g., an especially rough or degrading arrest). The conflict promoted by such actions may still not prove irreversible. Escalation may yet be prevented by reactions indicating that other members of the group, especially leaders, regard the original action as out of line.

Thus we were in the process of developing a model that seemed capable of explaining (though not always predicting) the relative likelihood of order or disorder as the outcome of a given event. A litmus test came with the Orgreave picket of May and June 1984.

Case Study 3:
The Orgreave Mass Picket, May–June 1984

Orgreave is the most complex of the case studies presented here. A mass picket rather than a demonstration, it lasted several weeks. Many academic commentators on the events at Orgreave have understandably focused on the worst day of violence, 18 June 1984.[25] However, the picketing of the British Steel Corporation coking plant began on 23 May with an attempt to discourage BSC from increasing the frequency of its daily coke supplies to its Scunthorpe steel plant above a quota already agreed between the NUM and steel unions.

With the exception of one ugly encounter on the first day, picketing initially consisted of little more than good-natured pushing and shoving. On Sunday 27 May, the NUM national president tried unsuccessfully to persuade local steel union officials to act in sympathy. As he emerged from the plant, the police dispersed pickets and bundled Scargill to the floor. This incident rankled with the miners.

Two days later (29 May), thousands of pickets congregated at Orgreave, to be confronted by police officers from eleven different forces.[26] One crowd of pickets, arriving unexpectedly early and assembling directly opposite the main gate, were charged by mounted police and dog handlers. A second group arriving later were contained half a mile from the gates by a police cordon. After a brief lull, the same sequence of events was enacted in the afternoon. The police claimed that the use of dogs and horses had been extemporised but others saw it differently: one local radio reporter described the manoeuvres as 'like a scene out of war, a battle' (BBC Radio Sheffield, 29 May).

The next day an initially small number of pickets swelled following the arrest of Arthur Scargill for obstructing the highway. Police and pickets charged into each other in scenes graphically captured by television cameras. On subsequent days, only a token picket was mounted. Then, on 18 June, the hundredth day of the strike, the NUM mounted a secretly organised mass picket of the plant which momentarily caught the police off guard. Dozens of pickets took advantage of the greatly reduced police presence to enter the coking plant, whence the police ejected them. A relatively minor confrontation between police and pickets occurred when the morning coke convoy arrived . Several accounts of the remainder of the day's events.[27] suggest that the police roadblock policy actually encouraged a build-up of miners at Orgreave.

The last confrontation on 18 June seemed, on the part of the police at least, to be a calculated and orderly re-enactment of the haphazard events of 29 May. ... Although their first sight of the massed ranks of the police officers, the way in which they were ushered into the area, given parking space, and almost a welcome aroused suspicion among some, most of the pickets awaited the arrival of the convoy in holiday mood. The struggle that followed was violent but unequal.[28]

Observers and analysts agree that the violence later that afternoon was precipitated by specific police tactics:

There is little evidence of stone-throwing before the first police advance. Indeed the official report is guarded. ... But as the official police film of the encounter makes clear (contrary to the image of much of the media coverage), there were no 'scenes of violence' before mounted police officers rode into the pickets and drove them away from the police line. Only after they had been attacked in this way did the pickets retaliate. Then barricades were built and set alight and missiles hurled at the advancing police.[29]

Proactive control of the crowd turned to retribution. Clad in riot gear, officers on foot followed in the immediate wake of their mounted colleagues 'with truncheons drawn, intent apparently more on injuring than taking prisoners'.[30] All such action appeared to be endorsed by the senior officers present. Ultimately, then, 'The police had clearly won the battle of Orgreave, but not without stirring up the miners' anger and leaving many with particular scores to settle later.'[31]

How far can the flashpoints model explain the events at Orgreave? To answer this question, we must consider the six levels of the model. At the *structural* level, the miners were becoming aware that they were taking on not just the National Coal Board but the Government and, increasingly, the police as their representatives. At the *political/ ideological* level, it had become apparent, 100 days into the strike, that the miners, vilified by government and the media, lacked powerful support. It was no coincidence that Orgreave took place at precisely the time that the isolation and thus determination of the miners was becoming most evident. At the *cultural* level, we encounter the heavily masculine ethos of both mining and police cultures, with their common but antagonistic commitment to protecting their own kind. *Contextual* factors included growing resentment against the police role, prior incidents on previous days' picketing, the sensitisation of the media to violence, and the total absence of any form of negotiation between protestors and police.

Most of all, the *situational* level provided cues for violence. There was a total incompatibility of objectives between pickets and police. The pickets wanted at least to talk to the lorry drivers and possibly obstruct their progress. The police had decided that they should not be allowed anywhere near them. Frustration thus met obduracy. The pickets were only loosely organised, while police tactics were improvised. In open space, the possibility of managing movement was minimal. The targets of derision for the miners switched from the drivers to the police. Each action was interpreted by the other side as justifying retaliation. Thus, at this *interactional* level, there was no possibility of accommodation in terms of norms governing behaviour. One 'flashpoint' almost inevitably followed another.

It is always easy in retrospect to construct an account which makes the outcome seem inevitable. However – and this is the claimed utility of the model – it is not always what is present, but rather what is *absent*, which remains crucial. At Orgreave, such absences included any mutual perception of each side as having certain rights to be respected, emergent norms on both sides of acceptable conduct, clear lines of authority and leadership amongst crowd and police, the perception of violence as counterproductive for either side; formal liaison between police and protestors, and recognition and defusion of provocative acts as potential flashpoints. Had all, or even *some*, of these been present, then violence might have been averted. What was absent at Orgreave turned out, upon examination, to be present at the large London demonstration some eight years later.

Case Study 4: The Hyde Park Rally, October 1992

The defeat of the year-long miners' strike in March 1985 enabled an unprecedented rate of pit closures. In the following seven years, 119 collieries were closed, with little public reaction. However, on 13 October 1992, the then Secretary of State for Trade and Industry, Michael Heseltine, committed the tactical miscalculation of announcing the Government's plans to close 27 collieries and 'mothball' a further four. The groundswell of opposition to this move spread well beyond the miners and their established supporters. Protests and demonstrations were held up and down the country, culminating in the Hyde Park rally.

Police policy towards this rally was strikingly different from that adopted during the 1984–5 dispute. Fundamental to this distinction was the dramatic change in public sympathy. With their industrial 'muscle' all but destroyed and their communities threatened by extinction, the image of miners and their families had been magically restored from 'scum' to 'salt' of the earth:

> The bungled announcement of the closure of thirty-one pits and 30,000 sacked miners triggered a spontaneous outburst of popular revulsion against the Government unprecedented in the Tories' fourteen years in office. Hertfordshire housewives wept into their washing-up, up to a quarter of a million people demonstrated in London twice in one week, Tory MPs were besieged by angry constituents and the Government was forced to retreat in the face of a backbench rebellion. Even Cheltenham marched for the demoralised miners, who emerged blinking into the light of unaccustomed media acclaim. For a fortnight, the miners' case was trumpeted around the land, the 'irrational' rigging of the energy market in favour of gas and nuclear power minutely explained and stoutly denounced. Arthur Scargill was transmogrified from most hated man in Britain into vindicated folk hero.[32]

The police were highly sensitised to the public mood:

> It was stressed during the briefing that officers should keep tight control of their teams and they were instructed to ignore the historical context – if the police had fought with the miners there would have been little public support or sympathy. The miners were almost totally supported by the public, conflict was to be avoided at all costs.[33]

P.A.J. Waddington's observations of pre-event negotiations between the NUM and the police confirm a spirit of co-operation. Both sides were concerned about the disruptive potential of a few 'hotheads'. The police accepted at face value NUM assurances that they were keen not to lose the 'moral high ground'. The NUM representative felt 'it was "good" for her to see that the police were not simply an arm of the government and were willing to pursue the interests of the NUM'.[34]

The miners' union was encouraged to appoint and brief its own stewards, with an investment in maintaining order. In return, the police obtained exceptional permission for the march to circumnavigate Hyde Park. A controversy over the potential use of police horses was defused by an agreement that they would be deployed but withdrawn immediately if they aroused hostility [35]. Such negotiations succeeded in producing a positive outcome:

> In the event, the demonstration was held in accordance with the arrangements negotiated. Cordial relationships were maintained, so

that when a radical group attended the march with a large banner on which was printed an obscene slogan, [a police] commander asked NUM stewards to have it removed. Several burly miners confronted the group, who were seen shortly afterwards, leaving the park with their offensive banner furled. Moreover, when another militant group staged a sit-down demonstration, stewards encouraged other demonstrators to continue. Another militant group did stage a breakaway march to Parliament Square, but were not supported by other demonstrators and were easily contained by police.[36]

The case of the 1992 demonstration in London thus indicates how subtle changes at one or more levels may be sufficient for the whole climate of the encounter to alter. In certain respects, 1992 was a continuation of 1984: it involved the same basis of conflict between miners' unions and a government determined to reduce (and, as we now know, to privatise) the mining industry. The same organisations (the NUM and the police) were in the front line with the whole conflictual history of the strike behind them. Moreover, the Metropolitan Police had been singled out as the most oppressive of all the forces policing the picket lines in 1984–5.

Such factors might superficially have created an expectation of potential disorder. Yet all these factors were counterbalanced by a subtle shift at just one of the levels of our model: the *political/ideological*. There was simply a different mood in government and, crucially, in public opinion. Mrs Thatcher had gone, ousted after the poll tax debacle. Her strident view of the 'enemy within' had been replaced by a much more moderate approach, in tone if not in deed. In any case, the miners and the trade union movement had been defeated. For the Government, there was no capital to be made from a show of force, especially because of the immediate (and, as it proved, ephemeral) groundswell of opinion in favour of the miners' cause. It would have been a foolhardy politician or police officer who failed to take into account this public mood, quite different from that during the original strike.

Though it still required specific actions by police and the NUM, in this sense an orderly outcome to the demonstration was consonant with the public mood. Disorder would have been counterproductive for police, miners and, arguably, government. Thus, it is the *political/ideological* level which most fully explains the actions of participants designed to avoid disorder at the 1992 demonstration. The low-key police approach seemed to run counter to what had otherwise been identified as the main trend in public order policing, towards paramilitary methods.

111

Paramilitary Policing: Definition and Process

The paramilitary approach to policing public disorder has been endorsed by Peter Waddington[37] and opposed by Tony Jefferson.[38] Waddington offers the more detailed definition, emphasising the use of protective shields and clothing by specialist units, trained in the use of squad formations and controlled force; intelligence gathering, surveillance and planning; and, crucially, the imposition of direct command and control by immediate senior officers. 'Instead of leaving individual officers to take uncoordinated action at their own discretion, a paramilitaristic approach deploys squads of officers under the direction and control of their own superiors.'[39] For Waddington, the development of a paramilitary approach was a response to political and industrial disorders in the 1970s and 1980s: 'It was not the police who abandoned consent in favour of coercion. The acquisition of this technology has been, at every stage, a *reaction* to the violence with which the police have been faced.'[40]

Jefferson's definition is less elaborate, 'namely, the application of (quasi) military training, equipment and organisation to questions of policing (whether under centralised control or not)'.[41] For Jefferson, the development of paramilitarism was part of a deliberate state strategy to forcibly suppress working-class protest and dissent. The tactical merits and shortcomings of the paramilitary approach are disputed. For Waddington, the emphasis on command and coordination is crucial in preventing police officers getting carried away in the heat of the moment:

> Policing civil disorder engenders fear, anger and frustration amongst officers who are often too close to the action to understand what is occurring. The feeling that one has lost control and is at the mercy of unpredictable events only heightens anxiety. The opportunity to take forceful action allows not only for the expression of these emotions, but is exhilarating in its own right. For all these reasons, it is essential that officers engaged in public-order situations are carefully supervised and controlled, for internal controls on behaviour are unlikely to prove reliable.[42]

If police officers are poorly trained, ill equipped and unsupervised, lacking clearly defined tactics or strategy, they may provoke as much disorder as they prevent. Disorganised forays by police officers undermine police legitimacy and incite the crowd. Disorder is less likely 'under paramilitary organisation comprising effective intelligence and trained personnel operating under hierarchical command in accordance with a formulated strategy and tactics'.[43]

Jefferson argues that paramilitarism has an 'inherent capacity to exacerbate violence'. Explaining this potential, he posits an 'ideal-typical sequential account' of the four distinct phases through which paramilitary methods are customarily deployed.[44] These are *preparation, controlling space, controlling the crowd* and *clearance.* In the *preparation* (or 'standby') phase waiting groups of officers exchange rumour, 'disparaging stories' about the enemy and 'precursory justifications' for their own imminent actions. The use of armoured police vehicles and personnel is inherently provocative.[45] Initial police attempts at *controlling space* – i.e., determining where the crowd may or may not stand – may easily create resentment, 'especially if the manner of clearance is with paramilitary shield and truncheon rather than more traditional forms of persuasion'.[46] Responses to such action confirm initial police expectations of trouble and harden their resolve.

When *controlling the crowd*, horses, dogs and riot shields may enhance the protestors' sense of grievance at 'the manifest injustice of heavily protected officers with truncheons drawn chasing defenceless members of the public'.[47] Sooner or later, snatch squads are bound to intervene, replete with

> the multiple protections of almost infinitely permissive public order law, a conception of supportive teamwork and an occupational culture which requires that the most aggressive and bull-headed individuals be supported in the field and defended in the aftermath, and an ideology of the demonstrator as violent sub-human undeserving of either respect or sympathy.[48]

This threshold passed, only a 'massive and highly oppressive police presence' can restore order.[49] Then follows the *clearance* phase. The police decide that the event is over and require the crowd to leave. Such arbitrary action will provoke more resistance. Even though the police will then appear to have secured their objectives, the cost will have been a further deterioration of relations with the protesting group.

P.A.J. Waddington counter-argues that Jefferson exaggerates the frequency and degree of force necessary. Control of crowds and space can be achieved by simple means: erecting barriers, cordoning off junctions and ushering people about. During 1990–1992, Waddington observed the planning and implementation of the Metropolitan Police's strategies and tactics at rallies and demonstrations in central London (including the infamous anti-poll tax riot of April 1990). He argues that, the more the police prepared for 'worst case scenario', the less likely disorder was. Only on those occasions when the police were *not* present in paramilitary strength did rioting occur: 'when significant numbers of police, including specialists in riot control, were deployed, there was progressively less violence'.[50]

Jefferson concedes that a paramilitary police presence reduces the likelihood of disorder but this is no justification in itself. Equally important is the aftermath, since 'perceived provocations which cannot be dealt with at the time do not disappear but linger on in collective folk memory ...[becoming] ... the backcloth against which future protests will take place and which will, in part, determine their outcome'.[51]

Paramilitary Policing: Outcomes and Prevalence

Peter Waddington has challenged the prediction that the police would use their increased powers under public order legislation to ban marches and demonstrations. The police seek to defend the democratic rights of protestors, whatever their cause. 'Indeed, instead of bowing to political pressure to ban marches, they actively resisted it, at what was perceived to be significant risk to individual careers.'[52] To explain their stance, Waddington evokes Chatterton's[53] notions of *trouble*. There are two types of trouble. *On the job trouble* is operational; it means having to use force and risking officers' safety. *In the job trouble* is political: the fallout of possible inquiries or investigations following controversial police action. These two are balanced out in police calculations. The prospect of *in the job trouble* can work either way. Sometimes it means the police must resort to firm measures, for example to protect symbols of the state such as Parliament or royalty. At other times, when protestors have some public sympathy or powerful allies, the prospect of *in the job trouble* might lead to an altogether more low key approach.

The general effect of the wish to avoid trouble of any kind gives police an occupational stake in the maintenance of order by the most efficient means.

> By avoiding confrontation and 'winning over' organisers they hope to escape both 'on the job trouble' in the guise of disorder and the 'in the job trouble' of inquiries and allegations of heavy-handedness and

provocation. Equally, if disorder erupts they want the 'insurance' of adequate preparation and reserves of personnel to quell the immediate trouble and demonstrate their capacity to do so.[54]

It is preferable to permit a controlled demonstration rather than risk controversy by banning or intervening in it. Pre-event negotiation is therefore designed to minimise disorder. Waddington recounts how experienced police negotiators utilise a wide repertoire of 'interactional practices and ploys' (such as exhibiting 'spurious friendliness' or extending helpful favours), and employ to their advantage various structural aspects of the negotiation (e.g., 'home-ground advantage' and their 'monopoly of expertise' about where protests can take place), to gain the compliance of the event organisers. Negotiation is largely one way, 'less a process of "give and take" and more of the organiser giving and the police taking. The police were enormously successful at ensuring that protest took place on their terms.'[55]

Jefferson and Grimshaw's more conceptual account suggests that senior police officers formulate their policies by taking into account the views of three significant 'audiences':[56] *legal audiences* (the courts, police authorities and the Home Secretary), *democratic audiences* (politicians and the community at large), and *occupational audiences* (more senior and junior officers). These audiences may give out similar or differing messages. The mass media are taken as a guide to the state of public, political and professional opinion.

Though differently conceptualised, both analyses stress the importance of the political context. In a democracy, the police must seek to maintain their legitimacy and formulate their policies accordingly. Paramilitary policing is regarded by all as an exceptional measure for which the appropriate cues must be available. That seems to us one convincing explanation of why paramilitary policing has not over the last fifteen years been used as often as it was in the miners' strike and the earlier inner-city disturbances. There are also at least two others.

Firstly, outside the exceptional case of Northern Ireland, mass protests are on the decline. Those groups who habitually used it, such as trade unions, students and ethnic minorities, have been politically marginalised. New social movements tend to eschew mass protests in favour of direct action, for example against road and airport developments. Although these pose public-order problems, they are of a quite different kind and require solutions which have little to do with crowd control.

Secondly, there has been a sea change in the general political atmosphere. Even before the election of a Labour government, the climate of confrontation and provocation associated with Margaret Thatcher had begun to decline. It was after all the policies of her government – over mine closures, the poll tax and the inner cities – which had themselves triggered mass political opposition. Subsequent governments have neither provoked nor sought to suppress popular protest.

This tends to validate Jefferson's model of the police as responsive to cues from their audiences, though this is not to deny that the police have their own occupational interests. Those audiences and their expectations have shifted: the route to paramilitary policing has been blocked. It is not a comprehensive answer to the problems of public order policing. Refinement of traditional methods is still required. We finally address these issues of police strategy, tactics and training in public order policing.

Police Policies and Practices

Here we outline the implications of our empirical and theoretical work for policing. We do not deny that there are two sides to this equation, that protestors and their leaders also have a role to play in the maintenance of order. Their acceptance of responsibility, eschewal of violence, provision of stewards and attempts to occupy the crowd are all vital. But ultimately the preservation of public order is the responsibility of the police. We now suggest the ways in which they can most effectively meet this objective by considering best practice under each heading of our 'flashpoints' model.

Our analysis consistently emphasises the *political/ideological* context as shaping the potential for disorder. The police should generally avoid taking sides in a conflict, as they did so lamentably in the miners' strike. The police should seek to be impartial in words as well as deeds. This requires senior police to avoid denunciations of the personnel or motives of protesting groups.

At the *cultural* level, police training should promote greater awareness, understanding and tolerance of the wide variety lifestyles and beliefs present in a modern, post-industrial democratic society. Aggressive beliefs and behaviours in the police occupational culture (notably the macho orientations to action, challenge, confrontation and control) should be displaced by an emphasis on peace-keeping. The composition of the force on the ground is important. The more local they are, the more they will be aware of long-term consequences of forceful intervention. There is also some evidence that the presence of female officers lessens the likelihood of confrontation.[57]

The police can play a key role at the *contextual level*. Set-piece events are far more likely to remain orderly when there is prolonged and meaningful negotiation and liaison between the police and the event organisers. The creation and maintenance of a 'contract with the crowd' is central to the preservation of order. The police should therefore cultivate any potential mediators between themselves and protestors.

Pre-event negotiation and agreements crucially affect the *situational level*. If mutual objectives are established beforehand, suspicion of each others' motives is less likely. The police should actively encourage the use of stewards, formal speeches and entertainment and permit non-violent symbolic expressions of grievance. It is also preferable to police demonstrations and picket lines by deploying small groups of 'traditionally' dressed police officers in a low-key manner with reinforcements kept out of sight. Clear lines of police communication and command are imperative. 'Situationally adjusted' officers, familiar with the mood of the crowd, are less volatile than loosely briefed Police Support Units arriving cold at the scene. Necessary police surveillance should be as low-key as possible. Traditionally uniformed officers communicating on two-way radios are less threatening than helicopters flying loudly overhead.

At the final *interactional* level, order is enhanced if the police adopt a flexible rather than rigid approach to minor breaches of the law, a tone which can be set in pre-event negotiation. Where force has to be used, it should be kept at the minimum necessary. Undue violence is always provocative.

Additional evidence to support these recommendations comes from Power and Tunstall who profiled thirteen instances of disorder in urban areas between 1991 and 1992.[58] A major problem was that the police had only a 'spasmodic presence' on the council estates where disorder occurred. Sudden, high-profile police interventions produced head-on confrontations between the police and local youths for control of the area. They conclude that police methods 'stressing street visibility, clarity and proactive policing', would have been more effective than reactive intervention.

We are therefore apt to agree with the call, by former Chief Constable John Alderson, for policing to be 'rooted in the community but not controlling people'. As he puts it,

Community policing demands specific skills including the ability to reason and articulate with the community. A good community police-man will know the area and problems of people on that patch. For those living in situations of deprivation, acting abnormally will be nor-mal behaviour for that individual – a good community policeman will know these factors and will use his or her discretion accordingly. A community police officer can't do this work unless he or she has the verbal skills to communicate, and the means to progress without vio-lence or use of force. The use of force and the criminal justice system is a last resort, almost a sign of failure in community policing.[59]

The recent diversification of the political agenda, with its greater accent on ecological, environmental and other moral issues (e.g. animal rights), has produced new social movements with innova-tive protest strategies and tactics.[60] Building a consensus for how such protests should be policed would seem an urgent task, from which recent trends in police organisation – towards militarisa-tion, privatisation and the introduction of performance indicators – seem a distraction. Nevertheless, it is to the principle of working with, and on behalf of, the whole of the community that the police should remain steadfastly committed.

Notes

1. *Morning Star*, 8 June 1984.
2. C. Lloyd, 'A National Riot Police: Britain's "Third Force"?' in B. Fine and R. Mil-lar (eds.), *Policing the Miners' Strike* (London, 1985), p. 70.
3. P.A.J. Waddington, *Liberty and Order: Public Order Policing in a Capital City* (London, 1994), p. 74.
4. D. Waddington, K. Jones and C. Critcher, 'Flashpoints of Public Disorder', in G. Gaskell and R. Benewick (eds.), *The Crowd in Contemporary Britain* (London, 1987); D. Waddington, K. Jones and C. Critcher, *Flashpoints: Studies in Public Disorder* (London, 1989).
5. Cf. P. Wilsher, D. MacIntyre and M. Jones, *Strike a Battle of Ideologies: Thatcher, Scargill and the Miners* (London, 1985).
6. N. Ridley, *My Style of Government* (London, 1991).
7. N. Lawson, *The View from Number 11* (London, 1992); P. Walker, *Staying Power* (London, 1991).
8. M. Thatcher, *The Downing Street Years* (London, 1993), p. 364.
9. Quoted in S. McCabe and P. Wallington, *The Police, Public Order and Civil Lib-erties* (London, 1988), p. 59.
10. J. McIlroy, '"The Law Struck Dumb"? – Labour Law and the Miners' Strike', in Fine and Millar (eds.), *Policing the Miners' Strike*.
11. Lloyd, 'A National Riot Police', in Fine and Millar (eds.), *Policing the Miners', Strike*, p. 65.

12. National Council for Civil Liberties (NCCL), *Civil Liberties and the Miners' Dispute* (London, 1984).
13. McIlroy, '"The Law Struck Dumb"?'; NCCL, *Civil Liberties and the Miners' Dispute*.
14. Quoted in McIlroy, '"The Law Struck Dumb"?', pp. 108–9.
15. NCCL, *Civil Liberties and the Miners' Dispute*.
16. R. Reiner, *Chief Constables: Bobbies, Bosses or Bureaucrats?* (Oxford, 1991).
17. P.A.J. Waddington, *The Strong Arm of the Law: Armed and Public Order Policing* (Oxford, 1991), p. 133.
18. P. Scraton, *The State of the Police* (London, 1985).
19. McCabe and Wallington, *The Police, Public Order and Civil Liberties*, p. 132
20. J. Alderson, 'A Fair Cop', *Red Pepper*, May 1996, p. 12.
21. South Yorkshire Police, *Policing the Coal Industry Dispute in South Yorkshire* (Sheffield, 1985).
22. D. Waddington, K. Jones and C. Critcher, *Flashpoints*, p. 182.
23. C. Critcher, 'On the Waterfront: Applying the Flashpoints Model to Protest against Live Animal Exports', and D. Waddington, 'Key Issues and Controversies', in C. Critcher and D. Waddington (eds.), *Policing Public Order: Theoretical and Practical Issues* (Aldershot, 1996); D. Waddington, *Contemporary Issues in Public Disorder: A Comparative and Historical Approach* (London, 1992); D. Waddington, K. Jones and C. Critcher, *Flashpoints*.
24. D Waddington, K. Jones and C. Critcher, *Flashpoints*, p. 167.
25. T. Jefferson, *The Case Against Paramilitary Policing* (Milton Keynes, 1990); G. Northam, *Shooting in the Dark: Riot Police in Britain* (London, 1988).
26. McIlroy, '"The Law Struck Dumb"?'.
27. See, inter alia, J. Coulter, S. Miller and N. Walker, *A State of Siege: Politics and Policing in the Coalfields* (London, 1984); B. Jackson and T. Wardle, *The Battle for Orgreave* (Brighton, 1986).
28. McIlroy, '"The Law Struck Dumb"?', p. 76.
29. Ibid, pp. 76–77.
30. Jefferson, *The Case Against Paramilitary Policing*, p. 97.
31. Ibid, p. 99.
32. *The Guardian*, 7 June 1993.
33. Metropolitan Police Superintendent, quoted in M. King and M. Brearley, *Public Order Policing: Contemporary Perspectives on Strategy and Tactics* (London, 1996) p. 82.
34. P.A.J. Waddington, *Liberty and Order*, p. 73.
35. Ibid., p. 74.
36. Ibid.
37. P.A.J. Waddington, 'Towards Paramilitarism? Dilemmas in the Policing of Public Order', *British Journal of Criminology* 27 (1987), pp. 37–46; idem, *The Strong Arm of the Law*; idem., 'The Case Against Paramilitary Policing Considered', *British Journal of Criminology*, 33 (1993), pp. 353–73.
38. T. Jefferson, 'Beyond Paramilitarism', *British Journal of Criminology* 27 (1987), pp. 47–53; idem, *The Case Against Paramilitary Policing*; idem, 'Pondering Paramilitarism: A Question of Standpoints?', *British Journal of Criminology* 33 (1993), pp. 374–88.
39. P.A.J. Waddington, 'The Case against Paramilitary Policing', p. 353.
40. P.A.J. Waddington, *The Strong Arm of the Law*, p. 217, original emphasis.
41. Jefferson, *The Case Against Paramilitary Policing*, p. 16.

42. P.A.J. Waddington, *The Strong Arm of the Law*, p. 137.
43. P.A.J. Waddington, 'The Case Against Paramilitary Policing Considered', p. 366.
44. Jefferson, 'Beyond Paramilitarism', pp. 51–3; idem, *The Case Against Paramilitary Policing*, pp. 84–6.
45. Jefferson, 'Beyond Paramilitarism', p. 51.
46. Jefferson, *The Case Against Paramilitary Policing*, p. 85.
47. Ibid.
48. Jefferson, 'Beyond Paramilitarism', p. 52.
49. Jefferson, *The Case Against Paramilitary Policing*, p. 85.
50. D. Waddington, *Contemporary Issues in Public Disorder: A Comparative and Historical Approach* (London, 1992), p. 362
51. Jefferson, 'Pondering Paramilitarism', p. 379.
52. P.A.J. Waddington, 'Coercion and Accommodation: Policing Public Order after the Public Order Act', *British Journal of Sociology* 40 (1994), p. 379.
53. M.R. Chatterton, 'The Supervision of Patrol Work under the Fixed Points System' in S. Holdaway (ed.), *The British Police* (London, 1979).
54. P.A.J. Waddington, 'Coercion and Accommodation', p. 379.
55. P.A.J. Waddington, *Liberty and Order*, p. 101.
56. T. Jefferson and R. Grimshaw, *Controlling the Constable* (London, 1984).
57. F. Heidensohn, 'We can Handle it out Here', *Policing and Society*, 4 (1994), PP. 293–303.
58. A. Power and R. Tunstall, *Dangerous Disorder: Riots and Violent Disturbances in Thirteen Areas of Britain, 1991* (York, 1997).
59. Alderson, 'A Fair Cop', p. 13.
60. King and Brearley, *Public Order Policing*; D. Waddington, 'Key Issues and Controversies'.

7

The Role of the Police:
Image or Reality?

Dominique Wisler and Marco Tackenberg

The question of the role of the police in controlling or provoking
civil disturbances cannot be reduced simply to the study of the
strategic interaction between demonstrators and the police. At this
micro level, police practices can make a substantial contribution to
the fate of a demonstration. The ethnographic study of London's
Metropolitan Police by P.A.J. Waddington describes the skills and
the wide repertoire of practices developed by police to control a
demonstration.[1] In the early 1970s, Rodney Stark formulated the
concept of 'police riot' to grasp the process by which police may
initiate a riot as a result of tactical failure and poor training.[2]
Patrick Bruneteaux, in his historical analysis of the French Gendarmerie, attributes the pacification of mass protest in France to
organisational and technical police innovation.[3] Police also can be
confronted – especially during waves of protest – with major tactical shifts by demonstrators and, through a process of adaptation,
have to learn how to regain control of a crowd.[4]

However, as we would like to argue here, there is another arena
where the demonstration battle is fought, namely the public
sphere.[5] At this level, a demonstration can be won or lost by police
once again. The portrayal of police practices in the mass media and
in the political field (in parliament, in public pronouncements of
the major political parties, in interviews with, or comments by,
prominent politicians), may be even more crucial for the develop-

ment of major occurrences of public disorder than the actual police action on the streets. In other words, the control by the police of public order is at best limited and their success or failure depends heavily on the reconstruction of the conflict in the public sphere.

Theoretical Considerations

Indeed, at the level of discourse, two opposing scenarios or 'frame packages' are always available after a public-order operation: first, the civil rights scenario, which repeatedly depicts the police as violent, brutal, provocative, uncontrolled, and the demonstrators' violence as a justified response of peaceful citizens to police provocation or failure; and second, the law and order scenario, which portrays police behaviour as correct, the use of force as necessary to restore the rule of law and as a response to the deliberate seeking of confrontation by organised and skilful extremist leaders and their blind followers. These scenarios are not necessarily grounded in the actual police operation on the streets, and the fact that specific media or political parties become active sponsors of one or the other of these scenarios is likely to result from other imperatives and considerations, such as electoral agendas.

Public-order operations are thus interpreted in the public sphere as disproportionate and brutal or, alternatively, as correct and tolerant, and this social reconstruction creates a set of constrains for both the police and the demonstrators, who are likely to orient their future action accordingly. Police action will constitute itself as response to their self-image produced in the public sphere. If a polemic about the use of public force arises in the media, the police are likely to become vulnerable to more criticism, and refrain, we would expect, from using indiscriminate force. The more powerful the civil rights coalition, the less likely are the police to flex their repressive muscle. This can be described as the *spotlight effect* of public scrutiny. If, by contrast, major newspapers and political parties sponsor a law and order frame package and the police become a 'blind spot' in the public sphere, then they may be encouraged and feel legitimised by the 'silent majority' to use more force to restore public order. On the protest side, a split in the public sphere would produce, as students of social movements have theorised, a 'window of opportunity' favourable to the development of further protest.[6] Once police become the focus of criticism for brutality or provocation, the demonstrators' sense of injustice finds greater resonance and more protest is the likely consequence.[7]

An initial violent demonstration may produce an immediate alignment of major sponsors behind one particular scenario in the public sphere. Alternatively, the two frame packages – civil rights and law and order – both may find strong sponsors for a particular event, thus creating a split in the public sphere and sharp debate. In general, the Left is more prone to adopt a civil rights frame package, while the conservative parties traditionally adopt a law and order perspective. During a protest wave, a shift in the sponsors' system may occur: one side may become 'silent' or sponsors may shift their allegiance to the alternative coalition. This is often described as a 'turning point' in a conflict, *Wende* in German.

Design of the Research

To illustrate the theory, we will discuss two cases of public disorders in Zurich, namely the Globus riot and the Opera riot. The first occurred in 1968, the second in 1980. The Globus riot was the first major instance of public disorder in Zurich since the mid 1950s. The police were unprepared and inadequately equipped, and they committed excesses that, theoretically, should have been translated into further protest. However, as we will see, this did not happen since the excesses were denied or underplayed in the public sphere by most political parties and journalists. As a result, tough – even unconstitutional – public-order measures could be taken without provoking a public outcry. By contrast, the Opera riot took place in a context of a much more professional police, better trained and equipped with riot gear. Despite the fact that the excesses of 1968 were not repeated, a controversy opened up. The public sphere was split by contradictory statements from major sponsors and, as a result, the conflict escalated for several months.

The position of the Social Democrats (PS) provides a measure of the strength of the civil rights coalition in Zurich. This is the biggest single political party in Zurich and monopolises the Left. The Communist Party and those of the New Left are insignificant in electoral terms, while the ecological party was established in the mid-1980s, after the period considered here. Since the strength of the civil rights coalition depends on the position of the Social Democrats, we will focus almost exclusively on the frame package used by this party as it is expressed in the city council debates held within ten days of the event, in the main mass media (*Tages-Anzeiger, Neue Zürcher Zeitung*), as well as in *Volksrecht*, the press organ of the PS in Zurich.

Within the media, the crucial newspaper is the *Tages-Anzeiger* (*TA*). The *Neue Zürcher Zeitung* (*NZZ*) is known invariably to sponsor the law and order frame packages. By contrast, the *Tages-Anzeiger*, which has a wider distribution,[8] is more liberal and more likely to adopt the civil rights frame package. While these are considered to be elite newspapers, there is a third major newspaper in Zurich – *Blick* – a tabloid paper which is comparable to the *Bild Zeitung* in Germany or the *Sun* in Britain. *Blick* is very agile, and can switch from one package to another overnight. While in both the Globus and the Opera riots *Blick* initially sponsored a civil rights frame package, it quickly modified its position in the later case and, in the protest wave that followed the Opera riot, adopted a decisive law and order frame package. To address the issue of the strength of the civil rights coalition in the media field, we will focus essentially on the position taken by the *Tages-Anzeiger*. Since the precise wording is very important to appreciate fully the position of the sponsors in the public sphere, we will include many of the original German quotations in the footnotes.

To be able to evaluate the *Wende* in terms of a shift from the spotlight to the blind spot, we have collected information on the size of the articles in the *Tages-Anzeiger* and the *NZZ* during the wave that followed the Opera demonstration (from June 1980 to December 1982). To measure the degree of scrutiny by political parties, we counted the number of interventions in the Zurich city council and identified their sponsors (coalition).

Before discussing these two cases, it is useful to define the notion of 'frame packages' and their components as well as to sketch the frame packages of the law and order and the civil rights coalitions as we can observe them over thirty years of public disorder in Switzerland.

Frame Packages

The notion of the frame, first discussed by Goffman,[9] has been developed by several authors to analyse political discourse.[10] A 'frame' is a centralising idea which focuses, selects, amplifies or condenses – in short, organises – experience in a particular way. Frames on political issues are clustered in a 'frame package',[11] and frame packages on public disorder contain at least five formal elements: scenario, antagonist and protagonists frames, as well as diagnostic and prognostic frames.[12]

The *scenario* describes suggestively the sequence of events during a demonstration as well as focusing on and selecting specific information. Thus, for example, a familiar and typical disagreement between the scenarios of two coalitions concerns the number of participants in a demonstration. Mann, in a study of liberal and conservative media reports on anti-(Vietnam)war mass demonstrations in the United States, found that the liberal media were likely to report a higher number of participants than the conservatives press.[13] The *protagonist* element of the frame package contains, in this case, the group and its sympathisers that are seen as advocating the demonstrators' goals and values or, in the case of the law and order coalition, the police and their sympathisers.[14] This frame makes attributions regarding the size of the group, or field of groups, its identity and its motives. The *antagonist* frame casts the group or field of groups seen as opposing either the movement or the police in the role of the villain. While the protagonist and antagonist frames make identity attributions, the *diagnostic* frame describes causality (of both the protagonists' and the antagonists' action) and attributes blame.[15] With regard to violent demonstrations, the diagnostic frame searches for the deeper causes which lie behind the violence. The diagnostic frame contains a *metaframe* that, in the case of public order, evaluates the legitimacy of the action of both police and demonstrators. Finally, the *prognostic* frame specifies what should be done and by whom, defining at the same time the goal, strategies and tactics. In the demonstration case, this involves the debate on what should be done to curb violence.

Two Alternative Images of Protest and the Role of the Police

From the analysis of nine violent demonstrations of left-libertarian movements and their reception in the Swiss public sphere, we can highlight the most important lines of the law and order and the civil rights frame packages according to the five formal elements of frames developed above.[16]

In the *scenario*, over and above the traditional disagreement between the two coalitions over the number of participants, there is a recurrent conflict over the interpretation of the chain of events leading to violence. The law and order coalition uses a 'programmatic model' which states that violence was planned by demonstrators or their leaders. The police, therefore, are cast in the role of 'being provoked', 'attacked by a hail of dangerous missiles', and their action always appears to be 'defensive'. The civil rights coalition disagrees strongly with this description and refers instead to an 'escalation model'. This portrays violence as spontaneous and unexpected; the police often play the role of an amplifier of violence, either because they react 'too early' or 'provoke' violence 'with their riot equipment'. Violence often is described as following a premature and unnecessary police manoeuvre towards a crowd. Both coalitions rhetorically exaggerate the violence of their respective antagonists and use euphemisms to describe their protagonists' action.

The law and order coalition displays a tendency to use an 'outsider model' to describe the *antagonist*. Accordingly, demonstrators are described as coming from 'outside the city' to riot, or as being 'foreigners'. Moreover, they are a 'minority', a 'small group' and they unjustly claim to represent a bigger social category (the 'nonrepresentativity model'). The law and order *antagonist* frame distinguishes between 'strategic leaders' and 'wire-pullers' on the one hand and 'blind', 'apolitical', 'irrational' followers on the other. The law and order *protagonist* frame claims that 'the vast majority' of the social group (youth for example) in fact opposes the goals of the demonstrators. They are the 'good youth', the 'rational ones', the 'responsible ones'. Demonstrators are not supported by the 'population at large', 'public opinion', or the 'real democrats'. The police are also cast by this coalition as protagonists. They are described as 'tolerant', 'patient', 'non-provocative', 'self-controlled'. Police must be 'thanked for their action'. Some policemen may sometimes 'loose their control', but this is explained by the 'heat of the moment'.

The representations of the protagonist and the antagonist of the civil rights coalition are almost the inverse mirror of the law and order frame package. Behind the values and goals of the demonstrators stands, according to the protagonist frame of this coalition, an entire social group. While this social group represents a 'minority' in society, it nevertheless has the support of 'public opinion' or, alternatively, of the 'real democrats'. The police are identified as the *antagonist* by the civil rights coalition. Very broadly, police are labelled through the 'amplification model'. The police, as a result of their culture, tactics or technology, help to amplify a conflict and are responsible for its escalation.

The main *diagnostic* frame of the law and order coalition employs a 'manipulation model' according to which riots are the artificial product of 'dishonest' leaders who 'lure' their 'naive' followers. The 'wires' that once led to the 'communist camp' today lead to 'anachronistic' or 'archaic' organisations. This manipulation model imports cold-war categories into the mass demonstration discursive field.[17] Most recently a new shift can be observed: increasingly the emphasis is on the 'fun' and 'excitement' that participants in a violent demonstration allegedly experience when 'fighting with the police'. From once being a 'strategic game', riot has become a 'game' tout court. Since, according to the law and order coalition, violence is basically the product of the agitation of a few leaders, the response to disturbances does not need to be political. Consequently the *prognostic* frame asks for more police and more efficient means to curb violence.

While the law and order coalition diagnoses the violence as the result of a (strategic) game, the civil rights coalition insists that strategic leaders are the symptom, not the cause, of violence. Riots, according to this coalition, are the exposed tip of an iceberg. Riots express the existence of a serious but neglected problem. Violence is the 'logical consequence' of long-term underlying structural changes. This coalition employs a 'social change model' to interpret violence. Consequently, the *prognostic* frame claims that the problem should be addressed. Dialogue rather than repression, political reforms rather than the status quo, are emphasised by the civil rights coalition. Police should 'disarm' and adopt a low profile rather than exacerbate the problem.

The Globus Riot

The Globus riot occurred on 30 June 1968. For several weeks, New Left organisations had attempted to channel the nascent cultural protest in Zurich into one demand: the establishment of an autonomous cultural centre in a municipal building left vacant by the departure of the Globus store chain. The movement was supported initially by left-wing and centrist politicians who had intervened in the city council with a motion to this effect. Paralleling these developments, the media spotlight had been aimed at the municipal police for several months. They had been accused of brutality and corruption. A cantonal judge was appointed by the authorities to investigate several affairs.

Faced with the authorities' opposition to their goal, the 1968 movement issued an 'ultimatum' and organised the so-called Globus demonstration. The event turned into a riot. There were over 160 arrests and many policemen as well as demonstrators were injured. Moreover, as was later confirmed by the cantonal judge mentioned above, arrested demonstrators experienced serious mistreatment by police.[18] However, crucially, this mistreatment was either denied or strongly underplayed by both the *Tages-Anzeiger* and the Social Democrats immediately after the event. The position adopted by the major potential sponsors of the civil rights frame package was crucial for the later course of the events.

The Frame Package of the *Tages-Anzeiger* and the Social Democrats

The reports in the *Tages-Anzeiger* and the statements issued by prominent Social Democrats after the event widely employed images drawn from the ideal-type of the law and order frame package. In the scenario, the initial police action was labelled as 'tolerant' and 'non provocative'. Moreover, the serious violence was attributed to 'left-wing rowdies' (*Radaubrüder*), suggesting a cold war model. Police were not identified as *antagonist*.

Let us illustrate this position first with statements of the *Tages-Anzeiger* and then with statements from the Social Democrats. In its first edition following the riot, the editorial of the *Tages-Anzeiger* framed the police as the *protagonist*: They were 'extremely tolerant', 'avoided any unnecessary provocation' (*vermied jede unnötige Provokation*), and 'demonstratively wore caps instead of helmets'.[19] The *Tages-Anzeiger* stressed that when police issued a 'warning' urging demonstrators to disperse, the 'ultimatum' was 'extended'. In the scenario, the *Tages-Anzeiger* oscillated between a 'programmatic model' and an 'escalation model' to explain the occurrence of violence. It insisted that the demonstration 'escaped the control of the organisers', but also emphasised that some groups were more organised. Thus, for example, it wrote: 'The first heavy missiles were used by demonstrators, whose strategy now seemed to be more organised and directed.'[20] More in line with the law and order frame package, some demonstrators were *antagonised* as 'shock troop' (*Stosstruppe*) of 'militant demonstrators, mostly left-wing youth'. Further, the *Tages-Anzeiger* used a 'manipulation model' by distinguishing implicitly between 'honest' and 'dishonest' youth. It suggested that the latter 'directed' the former.

Crucially, the first edition of the *Tages-Anzeiger* did not mention the alleged police brutality in its editorial dedicated to the riot. Buried deep on the third page of the three-page report, an article finished by pointing to the mistreatment and quoting some of the victims. The journalists, however, found the police excess excusable in the 'heat of the moment' and focused their criticism only on the beating of arrested demonstrators. This article remained the exception in the *Tages-Anzeiger*. As already noted, it was not mentioned in the editorial evaluating the police action, nor was it followed, in subsequent editions, by further comment or inquiry. Instead, the *Tages-Anzeiger* judged it useful to publish a statement signed by the entire editorial board, stating:

> The disorders of the last couple of days have created a situation that must be confronted with firmness and dignity. These characteristics have been displayed especially by those with political responsibility. The city council has shown with its public statements ... and with its most recent decree (ban on demonstrations) that it has understood what is necessary. One must recognise the honest effort of the police to control the difficult situations at demonstrations with skill and patience.[21]

The posture of the *Tages-Anzeiger* with regard to the police role during the Globus riot was very close to that of the *NZZ* and conservative politicians. The *NZZ* wrote, for example, that the police intervention was 'hard, but correct' and that, 'if in a few instances, one blow too many was given or unpleasant expressions were used by police, the responsibility clearly lay with the provocateurs'.[22]

The common posture of the *Tages-Anzeiger* and the *NZZ* did not remain unchallenged in the Zurich public sphere. *Blick* adopted a civil rights frame package. In the days following the Globus riot, *Blick* proved extremely critical of the police and repeatedly used strong metaphors such as 'beating-excesses like the Gestapo!', 'Gestapo-mentality', 'Gestapo-like beating orgy',[23] 'brutal revenge-justice of the police',[24] and, finally, 'blind action of the police'.

In the city council, however, the civil rights scenario found almost no sponsors. The Social Democrats joined the law and order coalition early on. The positions expressed by prominent members of the Party, such as Otto Lezzi, president of a local section of the Party,[25] and Alfred Messerli, president of the city council, fitted almost perfectly into the ideal-type of the law and order frame package. Thus, in a comment published by the *Volksrecht* (4 July

1968), Lezzi branded the demonstrators an 'unleashed pack of hounds' (*entfesselte Meute*), evoking through this animal metaphor an 'irrationality model'. Violence was described further as 'senseless'. Lezzi employed the 'non-representativity frame' and stated that the 'pack' was headed by 'a small, insignificant, but noisy minority' of 'negative forces' who misused (*missbrauchten*) the 'good youth' who came to demonstrate positively (manipulation model). These individuals 'came to Zurich' (outsiders model) to fight with the police (programmatic model). Lezzi acknowledged that the police intervention was 'hard, even very hard', but only to add immediately that this behaviour was 'understandable' (euphemism, legitimising frame) since 'beer bottles and other dangerous objects were thrown at the police' and, moreover, that the police often were acting in 'self-defence'.[26]

In a personal declaration before the council on 3 July and reproduced in the *NZZ*, Alfred Messerli made similar statements. He 'condemned' the 'bloody violence', stating that, indirectly, one person had died and about one hundred had been wounded (exaggeration, amplification of the demonstrators' violence). He insisted that he 'had repeatedly and clearly distanced [himself] from these extreme groupings'.[27] Further, he declared that this was the 'first time' that such violence occurred in Zurich (amplification), deplored that some policemen 'were wounded very severely in the exercise of their duty',[28] and, finally, 'thanked the police' who had 'fulfilled their duty in these turbulent days'.[29]

In a public statement regarding alleged police brutality, the Zurich trade unions joined the ranks of the law and order coalition. They judged the police violence to have been justified and legitimate since the demonstrators themselves were violent. They declared: 'Whoever makes use of violence has no right to be protected from violence himself.'[30] The Social Democratic faction adopted a somewhat softer frame in a declaration reproduced in most newspapers on 4 July, but also criticised the 'notorious rowdies' (*notorischen Radaumacher*). The faction also 'thanked' the police for their intervention but 'disapproved' (*missbilligt* – the wording is weak and remains short of a condemnation) of the fact that arrested demonstrators had been beaten up and wanted to distinguish between those demonstrators who came to protest and those who came to fight with the police (manipulation model).

The *Wende*

The adoption of the law and order frame package by most speakers in the public sphere was experienced by the Zurich municipal authorities as a *Wende* and by the movement as a 'pogrom climate'. Ernst Bieri, a conservative member of the Zurich government, made the following statement in the national daily *Der Bund* two days after the Globus riot:

> The passive population had to be shown who was really behind the 'active forces' who claim unjustly to speak for all youth. ... The reaction of the population is clearer today than three weeks ago. The vast majority of all political sides are indignant at the behaviour of a small group of left-wing extremists.[31]

In a later edition, the *NZZ* wrote: 'The events led to a clear shift in public opinion. After a phase of wide readiness in most circles for dialogue with the young critics of the "establishment", calls are now coming from all sides for an energetic restoration of public order.'[32]

Already in its edition of 1 July, the *Tages-Anzeiger* diagnosed such a turning point:

> The change in attitude that could be observed in the population for some time has turned into indignation. The main priority must be given now – by the honest youth as well as by the authorities and the press – to the efforts to bring about a climate of normality.[33]

This *Wende* allowed the authorities, as early as 2 July, to issue a general ban on demonstrations which lasted for two weeks. As noted above, this decision was welcomed by the *Tages-Anzeiger* editors on 3 July. Even though the measure was clearly unconstitutional, no organisation was prepared to take the administration to court. The *Wende* resulted in a climate of 'helplessness' (*Ratlosigkeit*) within the movement.[34] The civil rights activist Hermann Mohler diagnosed that 80 percent of the population was 'behind the government and the police'.[35] Mohler claimed further that the youth were 'deeply morally affected' and 'truly depressed' by what he and others had described as a 'pogrom situation'.[36] The movement demobilised immediately, and for several months not a single demonstration was organised by the student and youth movement in Zurich; the issue of an autonomous youth centre was more or less abandoned by the movement. The organisations behind the Globus demonstration dissolved themselves and, in the aftermath of the events, radicalisation occurred.[37]

The Opera Riot

The Opera riot took place on 13 May 1980 in the context of a referendum over a sixty-million-franc proposal for the renovation of the city's Opera. The proposal was supported by all parties, except the Social Democrats and the small Communist and New Left Parties. Their opposition was based on the argument that the Opera 'belonged' to a small elite, while nothing was being done for the popular culture. However, the Social Democrats were internally split. The trade-union wing of the Party, arguing that the renovation would create jobs, supported the proposal.

The Opera demonstration was organised by a committee that demanded a centre for the youth music subculture. The event, which turned violent, was the first of a long series of seventy-three, often violent, demonstrations which continued until April 1982. This wave, according to our hypotheses, was made possible by the immediate adoption by both the *Tages-Anzeiger* and the Social Democrats of a civil rights frame package. As criticism became quite vocal in the public sphere, the initially brutal police refrained from using force and the movement grew. Later in the protest wave a *Wende* occurred. When the Social Democrats and the *Tages-Anzeiger* turned the spotlight and criticism away from the police, the latter began to flex their repressive muscle on the streets. At the same time, the movement declined.

The Frame Package of the *Tages-Anzeiger* and the Social Democrats

The first article of the *Tages-Anzeiger* covering the Opera demonstration quoted only sources sympathetic to the movement. More in line with the traditional civil rights scenario this time, the *Tages-Anzeiger* adopted an escalation model to describe the sequence leading to violence. It wrote: 'Soon after the youths assembled in front of the main entrance of the Opera, a group of police, with shields and helmets, rushed in and *dispersed* [*wegtreiben*] the demonstrators.'[38] Similarly, *Volksrecht*'s scenario emphasised the peaceful character of the demonstrators in spite of the early police intervention which, as the journalist strongly suggested, had been provocative: 'The demonstrators sat in front of the Opera until the *armed* police intervened *without warning* from behind the building. *Nevertheless*, the demonstration still remained peaceful *for a long time*.'[39] Describing a subsequent demonstration by the movement, *Volksrecht* was more explicit in employing the provocation model: 'This time it was clear: the police provoked in vain.'[40]

The civil rights line adopted by both newspapers cited above can be highlighted by quoting the corresponding *NZZ* report on the same sequence of action:

> At 19:00 ... the main entrance was *occupied* so that Opera visitors were denied the entrance. At 19:28, the police decided to deploy its 30 *men*, who were sitting inside the building. Forming a cordon, they created a 'path' for the visitors, and the demonstrators were *somewhat* pushed back [*etwas zurückgedrängt*].[41]

The *NZZ* used legal wording to frame the demonstrators' action – they 'occupy' the entrance of the building; by contrast, the riot police intervention was described euphemistically – 'somewhat pushed back' (the *Tages-Anzeiger* had used the strong verb 'chase' instead) – and the riot equipment of the '30 men' was not mentioned. What sounded like a provocation of the riot police in the *Tages-Anzeiger* and *Volksrecht*, seemed in the *NZZ* article to be a routine operation by a few policemen based on the rule of law.

The alignment of the *Volksrecht* and the *Tages-Anzeiger* with the civil rights coalition is important. The framing activity deployed by these two newspapers contrasted markedly with their coverage of the Globus riot. During the latter the demonstrators, not the police, were labelled as 'provocateurs'; police, not demonstrators, were described as 'patient' and 'restrained'. With regard to the *diagnostic* and the *prognostic*, frame differences between the Globus and the Opera riot can also be emphasised. The diagnostic frame of both the *Tages-Anzeiger* and the Social Democrats, as expressed in *Volksrecht* and in some positions taken during the council debates, employed the 'structural model'. Speaking in the public sphere, Social Democrats identified a strong need for autonomy among the young and criticised the neglect of this problem by the administration. Ramer (PS), for instance, insisted on the 'urgency' of doing something for the young, while Zbinden (PS) argued that 'a lot of mistakes had been committed in the past, including by political parties and the administration'.[42] Another Social Democrat expressed his disapproval of 'those who want to push the rule of law even when the world is crumbling'.[43] *Volksrecht* declared: 'They [the young] are still waiting – since the Globus riot – for a youth centre.'[44] In addition, commenting on the initial refusal of the authorities to negotiate under the pressure from the streets and violence, an editorial of the *Volksrecht* declared: 'Those who react only when cobblestones are thrown should not be surprised when cobblestones are indeed thrown. ... When did the Zurich authorities talk with the young?'[45] Typical of the prognostic of the civil rights frame package, the Social Democrats and the *Tages-Anzeiger* advocated dialogue and reforms. Repression was no longer seen as an appropriate answer to social change.

The *Wende*

As in the Globus case, but much later in the wave, there was a *Wende*. The Zurich police observed the shift of public opinion with great relief, as is attested by an interview we conducted with the chief of the cantonal security police at that time:

> At the beginning of the 1980s, the cantonal parliament was not interested in what happened in Zurich. That was the city, and there the pressure of the Left on the police was tremendous. It was said that there was a need to let them articulate their demands, and so on. And then slowly came the pressure of the right. ... This we [in the police] could witness, and we received a strong back up.[46]

Further:

> The more demonstrations occurred in the [early] 1980s, the more pressure was exerted from the Right: 'Now you must do something'; the 'citizens are fed up'; 'now you have to finish this business', and so on. ... At the beginning we probably waited too long. In principle we tolerated all demonstrations. We said the official demonstration will be tolerated, but no illegal ones and, when they happened, we tolerated them anyway. On the demonstrators' side, this behaviour created the feeling that we would not intervene and that the streets belonged to the movement. The turning point occurred *less from a shift in police tactics than from a shift in public opinion*. The population was fed up. The demands of the movement were more or less all satisfied. 'What do they want?'; 'It is only a question of a show of power in the streets?'; 'they comprise small groups!' Of course, in the police we observed this shift and, of course, we could feel that public opinion was now backing us.[47]

The *Wende* in the Council and the *Tages-Anzeiger*

According to our hypotheses, police perception depends on the images produced in the public sphere. To address the issue and the timing of the shift of public opinion in the public sphere, we refer to the periods of protest wave highlighted in Kriesi's analysis on the 'Autonomen' movement in Zurich.[48] The first period extended from the Opera riot and the opening by the city of an autonomous centre to its first closure on 7 September 1980. There then followed a period of renewed mobilisation of the movement until the reopening of the centre on 3 April 1981. The third period lasted until 12 October 1981, when the centre was closed once again. The final period, described by Kriesi as a 'destruction phase', lasted until the elections of March 1982. These elections definitively closed the door on the movement by giving the law and order coalition a clear-cut success.

In the city council, the turning point seems to have resulted less from a defection of the Social Democrats than from an increasingly vocal law and order coalition. Table 1, which displays by period the number and distribution of interventions in the city council according to the frame package supported, allows two observations. First, it is only in the third period (with the reopening of the centre) that the Left remained entirely silent. In fact, after the reopening of the centre, the Social Democrats made only one intervention (in the fourth phase). The 'pressure from the Right' already had mounted in the second phase. Second, we can observe that public order ceased to be an issue in the council arena after the reopening of the centre. While on average every second demonstration was likely be echoed in the council during the first two phases, only one out of ten was debated during the last two periods. Ironically, as we will show below, public order operations were no longer the focus of public scrutiny at the very moment when the level of repression in the streets increased.

Table 1. *Interventions in the Zurich City Council from two coalitions during the protest wave, by period (June 1980 to April 1982)*

Period	Law and Order	civil Rights/Left	Total Number
1. First Centre	2	8	10
2. Remobilisation	6	10	16
3. Second Centre	2	0	2
4. Dissolution	0	2	2

It is worth adding that while council interventions usually were followed by a debate, the last interventions were met with total silence from the deputies of the other parties, including the Social Democrats. Moreover, while the responses of the government in 1980 usually took up several pages in the proceedings, they became laconic in 1982. Each written question was answered with one or two sentences. Silence deepened around the movement.

What about the coverage by the newspapers? To discuss what was highlighted (or ignored) in the public sphere, we examined the coverage by the *Tages-Anzeiger* and the *NZZ* (see Table 2). Not only did the coverage rate of the *NZZ* diminish somewhat from one period to the next, but, more interestingly, the articles became shorter and shorter. This cannot be explained by a diminishing news value of the events since, in fact, protesters' violence increased as did the use of force by the police. A similar pattern is visible in the *Tages-Anzeiger*. The spotlight of the media was clearly on the movement at the beginning of the protest wave, but as the wave evolved, so the movement became more and more a blind spot. In general, however, the *Tages-Anzeiger* covered the protest wave more extensively than the *NZZ*.

Table 2. *The Press coverage of the protest wave by period (June 1980 to May 1982)*

Period	Coverage Rate of the NZZ (percent)	Mean size of the NZZ articles[1]	Mean size of the TA articles[1]
1. First Centre	93.7	0.66	1.03
2. Remobilisation	81.2	0.33	0.44
3. Second Centre	68.7	0.25	0.33
4. Dissolution	75.0	0.13	0.43

1. Percentage of a full-size page

The *Wende*, the Police and the Demonstrators

How did this evolution in the public sphere affect police behaviour? How did police react to the spotlight of public scrutiny during the early phase of the movement and its weakening during the later phases? As mentioned above, the police observed the shift of public opinion, but how did this perception translate into action?

To discuss patterns of repression during the protest wave we use three different measures of police coercion. When police use force to stop a peaceful march, the police action can be labelled as legalist; police action is clearly repressive when force instead of toleration is applied during a protest; ultimately, police can use rubber bullets to disperse a march. Rubber bullets have been a target of public criticism since their initial use during the Opera riot. As a controversial means of coercion, the use of rubber bullets by police is a good indicator of the level of repression applied to a movement.

Table 3. *Police use of force during the protest wave by period (June 1980 to May 1982), in percentage*

Period	Legalism[1]	Repression[2]	Rubber Bullets[3]
1. First Centre	30.8	43.7	55.5
2. Remobilisation	35.5	50.0	66.6
3. Second Centre	25.3	64.7	83.3
4. Dissolution	75.0	87.5	100

1. Percentage of police use of force in case of illegal but peaceful demonstration
2. Percentage of police force in case of illegal violent deomonstration
3. Percentage of use of rubber bullets in case of police use of force

Police became more legalist and repressive, and increasingly used rubber bullets during the protest cycle (Table 3). As compared to the first period, the level of force increased by a factor of two for all indicators. While rubber bullets were used in every second police intervention during the first period, they are used in all instances during the last. Indeed, after an initial intervention which triggered the Opera riot, the police seemed to hesitate between repression and toleration until about the beginning of the third period, which corresponds with the reopening of the centre. From this time onwards, repression became the usual choice for police when confronted with public disorder.

The hesitation of the police, their moderate use of rubber bullets and frequent toleration of public disorder during the first two periods, can be explained by the spotlight effect of the public sphere. This initial caution mirrors the degree of public scrutiny. The police, although supported by the *NZZ*, was the focus of harsh criticism in the *Tages-Anzeiger* at the beginning of the cycle. For instance, when the police intervened with a massive use of tear gas to disperse a unauthorised march on 18 June 1980 they were accused by the *Tages-Anzeiger* of having committed tactical mistakes. The newspaper focused its report almost exclusively on the police wrongdoing and produced a full page of comment. The editorial of the *Tages-Anzeiger*, written by the editor-in-chief, was suggestively titled 'Not like this!' (*So nicht!*).

As the object of criticism from a large initial civil rights coalition, the police became vulnerable and hesitant, and refrained most of the time from using excessive and controversial force. As the situation shifted in their favour in the middle of the cycle, so repression increased. During the dissolution phase of the wave, as press coverage diminished, the police resorted to their most controversial means – rubber bullets – and systematically dispersed any march, peaceful or violent. Moreover, they declared any march illegal and refused to give new permits to sympathisers of the movement. As mentioned earlier, the increase of repression did not stimulate journalists to cover the events (as we otherwise would have expected given their professional values), and this could be interpreted by police as an additional sign of the legitimacy of their new repressive course.

As protest became more or less a blind spot in the media and the law and order scenario won in the city council, the nature of protest changed (see Table 4). It grew increasingly militant, while many earlier participants left the movement. By the end of the cycle, two thirds of public demonstrations ended in violence. This violence can be explained as a reaction to the closure of the public sphere and the related increased in police repression. As the costs of mobilisation increased (the rubber bullets led to five demonstrators losing an eye), less militant participants abandoned the actions. From an average of 600 demonstrators in the initial phase of the movement, the number stabilised at about 200 militants during the last two phases.

Table 4. *Mobilisation and violence levels during the protest wave by period (June 1980 to May 1982)*

Period	Violence (in percent)	Median Number of Demonstrators	Number of Demonstrations by Month
1. First Centre	56.2	600	5.3
2. Remobilisation	59.4	300	4.6
3. Second Centre	70.6	175	2.8
4. Dissolution	75.0	250	1.3

Conclusion

In this paper, we have tried to demonstrate that police behaviour during major cases of public disorder cannot be understood adequately merely in terms of the interactive dynamics with protesters on the streets but depends heavily on the images produced in the public sphere. Depending on which scenario 'wins' in the public sphere, the police may be weakened or strengthened and, correspondingly, protesters encouraged or discouraged from continuing with their protest. Police reconstruct their identity and their legitimacy in the light of the discursive alignments produced in the public sphere. When they observe that the spotlight of the media has been switched off and feel that the right-wing politicians have won the symbolic battle, they consider it legitimate to flex their repressive muscle and, as was the case during the Opera wave, may begin to use coercive means otherwise considered controversial. Likewise, protesters react to the frame alignments in the public sphere. In the two cases analysed here, the closure of the mass media induced a dual process of demobilisation and radicalisation.

The 'patterns of provocation' in the frame packages of the two coalitions are so robust and so persistent over time that we suspect that they have more to do with ready-to-use scenarios, available as a cultural heritage to journalists and other commentators in the public sphere, than with the riot itself. The actual police behaviour in the streets resembles the 'shadows' in Plato's myth of the cave; the essential 'things' are the ideas, the civil rights and law and order frame packages, that journalists, leader writers, politicians and perhaps even social scientists use routinely to reconstruct events which, most of the time, they have not witnessed personally.

To understand the dynamics of a protest wave it becomes crucial to identify the conditions of the success of a scenario in the public sphere. Under what conditions does the law and order or the civil rights coalition win the symbolic battle? Responding to this empirical question is likely to improve our understanding of the actions and reactions of both the police and protesters. Our discussion of the Globus and the Opera riots provides some evidence that the adoption of a particular scenario is not necessarily linked to evidence from the outside world. Allegations of brutality in the Globus case were publicly denied by most speakers despite, as became evident later, their truth. In the Opera riot, police provocation was dramatised by major sponsors – the *Tages-Anzeiger* and the Social Democrats at the forefront – and this created ideal conditions for the development of the mobilisation.

The question of the condition of success of a scenario within the public sphere is a difficult one that needs to be addressed by further research. We can offer only two suggestions on this topic. First, social change was certainly responsible for the opening of the public sphere in the 1980s in Switzerland. Since the two waves of protest in Switzerland, new social movements have come to be recognised as a strong element of democracy and the police institution has become more closely controlled by public opinion. Second, electoral politics remain crucial factors. Enduring violence during the 1980 protest wave and fear by the Social Democrats that they might have to pay a heavy price for their unconditional support in the March election were responsible for their growing silence at the end of the wave. In fact, these fears were quite legitimate since the conservatives made significant advances in the elections two years later.

Notes

1. P.A.J. Waddington, *Liberty and Order: Public Order Policy in a Capital City* (London, 1994).
2. Rodney Stark, *Police Riots: Collective Violence and Law Enforcement* (Belmont, Calif, 1972).
3. Patrick Bruneteaux, *Maintenir l'ordre. Les transformations de la violence d'État en régime démocratique* (Paris, 1996).
4. Doug McAdam, *Political Process and the Development of Black Insurgency, 1930–1970* (Chicago, 1982); Dominique Wisler and Hanspeter Kriesi, 'Public Order, Protest Cycles and Political Process: Two Swiss Cities Compared', in Donatella della Porta and Herbert Reiter (eds.), *Policing Protest: The Control of Mass Demonstrations in Western Democracies* (Minneapolis, 1998).
5. We use the concept of public sphere to denote the mass media as well as parliamentary debates (in so far as they are reproduced in the mass media).
6. Charles Tilly, *From Mobilization to Revolution* (Reading, Mass., 1978); McAdam, *Political Process*; Sidney G. Tarrow, *Struggle, Politics and Reform: Collective Action, Social Movements and Cycles of Protest* (Ithaca, N.Y., 1991).
7. See McAdam, *Political Process*; William A. Gamson, *The Strategy of Social Protest* (Belmont, Calif., 1975).
8. Whereas the *NZZ* today has a circulation of about 150,000, that of the *Tages-Anzeiger* approaches 300,000.
9. Erving Goffman, *Frame Analysis: An Essay on the Organization of Experience* (Cambridge, Mass., 1974).
10. David A. Snow and Robert D. Benford, 'Master Frames and Cycles of Protest', in Aldon D. Morris and Carol McClurg Mueller (eds.), *Frontiers in Social Movement Theory* (New Haven, 1992); A. Scott Hunt, Robert D. Benford and David A. Snow, 'Identity Fields: Framing Social Processes and the Social Construction

of Movement Identities', in Enrique Laraña, Hank Johnston and Joseph R. Gusfield (eds.), *New Social Movements: From Ideology to Identity* (Philadelphia, 1992); Donatella della Porta, *Social Movements, Political Violence, and the State: A Comparative Analysis of Italy and Germany* (Cambridge, U.K., 1995); Donald A. Schön and Martin Rein, *Frame Reflexion: Toward the Resolution of Intractable Policy Controversies* (New York, 1994); William A. Gamson, *Encounters with Unjust Authority* (Homewood, Ill., 1982); David A. Snow and Robert D. Benford, 'Ideology, Frame Resonance and Participant Mobilization', *International Social Movement Research* 1 (1988), pp. 197–217.

11. William Gamson and André Moddigliani, 'Media Discourse and Public Opinion on Nuclear Power: A Constructionalist Approach' *American Journal of Sociology* 95 (1989), pp. 1–37.

12. See Donatella della Porta, 'The Political Discourse on Protest Policing: Italy and Germany from the 1960s to the 1980s', in Marco Giugni, Doug McAdam and Charles Tilly (eds.), *How Social Movements Matter* (Minneapolis, 1999). Several studies have discussed the coexistence of different representations of protest in the media in general. Douglas M. McLeod and James K. Hertog, 'The Manufacture of "Public Opinion" by Reporters: Informal Cues for Public Perceptions of Protest Groups', in *Discourse and Society* 3 (1993), pp. 259–75, find contrasting discourses between what they call 'mainstream media' and alternative media' in reporting on an anarchist mass demonstration in Minneapolis. Hanspeter Kriesi, *Die Zürcher Bewegung. Bilder, Interaktionen, Zusammenhänge* (Frankfurt am Main, 1984), shows that during a protest wave there actually always are three representations in the public sphere: one from the antagonists of the movement, one from the sympathisers of the movement, and one from the movement itself. Della Porta, *Social Movements*, reconstructs the ideal-types of the frame packages used by the civil rights and the law-and order coalitions with regard to the violent mass demonstrations of left-libertarian movements in Germany and Italy.

13. Leon Mann, 'Counting Crowd Effects of Editorial Policy on Estimates', *Journalism Quarterly* 101 (1974), pp. 278–85.

14. A. Scott Hunt, Robert D. Benford and David A. Snow, 'Identity Fields'.

15. Snow and Benford, 'Ideology, Frame Resonance and Participant Mobilization', p. 200.

16. See also Marco Tackenberg, 'Discourse on Protest: A Comparative Frame Analysis on Protest Events in Three Swiss Cities from 1968 to 1996' (Master's thesis, University of Geneva, 1997).

17. See, for example, Dabiel Hallin's study of the media and Vietnam in the United States: Daniel C. Hallin, *The 'Uncensored War': The Media and Vietnam* (Berkeley, 1986).

18. See the response of the Zurich municipal government to the intervention in the city council, in W. Kull et al., *Protokoll des Stadtrates von Zürich*, 6 December 1968. See also the response of the Zurich municipal government to the intervention, in O. Lezzi and J. Lechleiter, *Protokoll des Stadtrates von Zürich*, 10 October 1968.

19. *TA*, 1 July 1968.

20. *TA*, 1 July 1968.

21. Die Unruhen der letzten Tage haben eine Situation geschaffen, der mit Festigkeit und Würde begegnet werden muss. Diese Eigenschaften haben vor allem die in politischer Verantwortung Stehenden zu beweisen. Der Stadtrat hat mit seinen Verlautbarungen – so der Appell des Stadtpräsidenten – und mit seiner neuesten Verfügung (Demonstrationsverbot) gezeigt, dass er das Gebot der

Stunde verstanden hat. Der Polizei darf das ehrlich Bemühen attestiert werden, die schwierigen Situationen an den Demonstrationszentren mit Geschick und Geduld zu meistern. *TA*, 3 July 1968.

22. Wenn in einzelnen Fällen ein Schlag zu viel gegeben wurde und auch Polizisten unschöne Worte brauchten: diesmal liegt die Schuld daran eindeutig bei den Provokateuren. *NZZ*, 1 July 1968.
23. Prügel-Orgie wie bei der Gestapo!
24. Brutale Rachejustiz der Polizei. *Blick*, 4 July 1968.
25. Otto Lezzi was president of the Party section in electoral district seven of the city of Zurich.
26. Es trifft zu, dass die Polizei sehr oft in der Lage der *Selbstverteidigung gestanden hat. Die Feststellung darf und muss gemacht werden.* (Lezzi, in *Volksrecht*, 4 July 1968) .
27. Ich habe mich immer wieder eindeutig gegen diese extremen Gruppierungen abgegrenzt.
28. In der Ausübung ihrer Pflicht zum Teil sehr schwer verletzt worden sind.
29. Messerli, in *NZZ*, 4 July 1968.
30. Wer Gewalt anwende, hat keinen Anspruch darauf, vor Gewalt geschützt zu werden. *NZZ*, 5 July 1968.
31. *Der Bund*, 2 July 1968.
32. *NZZ*, 7 July 1968.
33. Die schon seit einiger Zeit in der Bevölkerung feststellbare Veränderung hat sich zur Empörung gesteigert. Die vornehmste Aufgabe – sowohl der ehrlichen strebenden Jungen als auch der Behörden und der Presse – muss daher auf das Bemühen gerichtet sein, eine Atmosphäre der Normalität herbeizuführen. *TA*, 1 July 1968.
34. Hanspeter Kriesi, *Die Zürcher Bewegung*, p. 187.
35. Interview with Hermann Mohler, *Weltwoche*, 9 August 1968.
36. Viele haben eine eigentliche Depression. See also Otmar Hollstein, quoted in Kriesi, *Die Zürcher Bewegung*, p. 186.
37. See Dominique Wisler, *Drei Gruppen auf der Suche nach der Revolution* (Zürich, 1996).
38. Kurz nachdem sich die Jugendlichen vor dem Haupteingang des Opernhauses aufgestellt hatten, drang ein mit Schutzschildern und Helmen versehendes Aufgebot der Stadtpolizei aus dem Opernhaus und trieb die Demonstranten weg. *TA*, 2 June 1980, our italics.
39. *Volksrecht*, 6/7 June 1980, our italics.
40. Diesmal war es eindeutig: Provoziert hat die Polizei vergeblich. *Volksrecht*, 6/7 June 1980.
41. *NZZ*, 2 June 1980, our italics.
42. Debate, in *NZZ*, 26 June 1980.
43. Debate, in *NZZ*, 26 June 1980.
44. Sie verfügt auch 12 Jahre nach dem Globus-Krawall noch über kein eigenes Jugendhaus. *Volksrecht*, 2 June 1980.
45. Wer nur auf Pflastersteine reagiert, darf sich nicht wundern, dass Pflastersteine fliegen. ... Wann haben die Zürcher Behörden mit den Jugendlichen gesprochen? *Volksrecht*, 6/7 June 1980.
46. Interview with Major Heinz Hugi, 9 March 1995.
47. Interview with Major Heiz Hugi, 9 March 1995.
48. Kriesi, *Die Zürcher Bewegung*, p. 40.

A Note on Further Reading

The endnotes to the chapters provide the most comprehensive guides to further reading of the topics discussed in this volume. The number of references to primary source material is an indicator of how few historical monographs have addressed these issues. While, since the 1960s, historians have undertaken considerable research into riots and rioters, and especially for the pre-industrial period, there has been very little historical work on the forces responsible for controlling disorder, and the impact of their behaviour on the course of disorder. This latter, in contrast, has generated considerable interest and controversy among sociologists and criminologists. The sharpest debate in the English language is that between Tony Jefferson and P.A.J. Waddington and best explored in their respective books, *The Case Against Para-Military Policing* (Buckingham, 1990) and *The Strong Arm of the Law. Armed Police and Public Order Policing* (Oxford, 1991). P.A.J. Waddington, *Liberty and Order: Public Order Policing in a Capital City* (London, 1994) is also useful as a sympathetic account of the Metropolitan Police planning for, and responding to the exigencies of the moment in, a variety of public demonstrations and celebrations during the early 1990s. David Waddington, Karen Jones and Chas Cricher, *Flashpoints: Studies in public disorder* (London, 1989), amongst other things, offers a more critical account of some police activity. On the comparative side, there are some useful introductory essays in John Roach and Jürgen Thomaneck, eds. *Police and Public Order in Europe* (London, 1985); and for the French Police in particular see Christine Horton, *Policing Policy in France* (London, 1995).

Roger Geary, *Policing Industrial Disputes: 1893-1985* (Cambridge, 1985) addresses the shifting tactics of the English police in dealing with industrial protest. Jane Morgan, *Conflict and Order: The Police and Labour Disputes in England and Wales, 1900-1939* (Oxford, 1987) and Barbara Weinberger, *Keeping the Peace? Polic-*

ing Strikes in England and Wales 1906-1926 (Oxford, 1991), address similar issues over a shorter time span, with a less schematic approach. They also focus closely on official sources, such as Home Office minutes and papers, and while this helps understand the view from Whitehall and the chief constable's office, it does not address the perspective of the policeman on the street confronting a crowd. Some pointers towards the view and behaviour of the policeman on the street can be found in Clive Emsley, 'Police Forces and Public Order in England and France during the Inter-War Years' in Clive Emsley and Barbara Weinberger, eds. *Policing Western Europe: Police, Professionalism and Public Order, 1850-1940*, (Westport, Ct., 1991).

There are general histories of English and French police which touch on some of these issues; for example, Clive Emsley, *The English Police; A Political and Social History* (2nd. edn. London, 1996), and Philip John Stead, *The Police of France*, (London, 1984). For Germany see Hsi-Huey Liang, *The Berlin Police Force in the Weimar Republic* (Berkeley, Los Angeles and London, 1970); Richard Bessel, 'Policing, Professionalisation and Politics in Weimar Germay', in Emsley and Weinberger, Policing Western Europe, and also his 'Police and Society in Eastern Germany after 1945', *German History*, 10 (1992); Herbert Reinke, 'The Policing of Politics in Germany from Weimar to the Stasi', in Mark Mazower, ed., *The Policing of Politics in the Twentieth Century* (Providence and Oxford, 1997). The best introductory guide to police in the United States is the bibliographical essay by Eric H. Monkkonen, 'The Urban Police in the United States', in Clive Emsley and Louis A. Knafla, *Crime Histories and Histories of Crime: Studies in the Historiography of Crime and Criminal Justice in Modern History* (Westport, Ct., 1996), and see also, Michael W. Flamm, *Law and Order: Street Crime, Civil Disorder, and the Crisis of Liberalism* (New York, forthcoming).

Contributors

Richard Bessel is Professor of Twentieth-Century History at the University of York and coeditor of the journal *German History*. He is the author of *Germany after the First World War* (Oxford: 1993), and the editor of *Fascist Italy and Nazi Germany: Comparisons and Contrasts* (Cambridge: 1996), and, with Ralph Jessen, *Die Grenzen der Diktatur. Staat und Gesellschaft in der SBZ und DDR* (Göttingen, 1996).

Chas Critcher is Professor of Communications and Head of the Communications, Media and Communities Research Centre at Sheffield Hallam University. He has been a long-time collaborator with David Waddington on policing matters, notably coediting *Policing Public Order: Theoretical and Practical Issues* (Aldershot, 1995). They also worked together on *Redundancy and After: A Study of Ex-miners from Thurcroft in the Aftermath of Pit Closure* (Sheffield, 1995) and *Split at the Seams? Community, Continuity and Change after the 1984–5 Coal Dispute* (Milton Keynes, 1990).

Andrew Davies is Lecturer in the School of History at the University of Liverpool. He is the author of *Leisure, Gender and Poverty: Working-Class Culture in Salford and Manchester, 1900–1939* (Buckingham, 1992) and is currently working on a project on street gangs and violence in British cities from the 1870s to the 1930s.

Clive Emsley is Professor of History at the Open University and, currently, President of the International Association for the History of Crime and Criminal Justice. His publications include *The English Police: A Political and Social History* (London, 2nd ed. 1996) and *Gendarmes and the State in Nineteenth-Century Europe* (Oxford, 1999).

Michael W. Flamm is Assistant Professor of History at Ohio Wesleyan University. He is the author of *Law and Order: Street Crime, Civil Disorder, and the Crisis of Liberalism* (Columbia University

Press, forthcoming). He has also published articles in the *Journal of Policy History* and *Agricultural History*.

Simon Kitson is Lecturer in French at the University of Birmingham. He has published several articles on policing in France since the 1930s and is currently preparing a monograph on the French Police from the Popular Front to the Liberation with a particular focus on Marseilles.

Peter Leßmann-Faust is currently Deputy Director of the Informations- und Bildungszentrum, Schloß Gimborrn. His publications include *Die preußische Schutzpolizei in der Weimarer Republik. Streifendienst und Straßenkampf* (Düsseldorf, 1989) and 'Geschichte der Polizei', in Michael Kniesel, Edwin Kube and Mandfred Murck (eds.), *Handbuch für Führungskräfte der Polizei. Wissenschaft und Praxis* (Essen, 1996).

Marco Tackenberg is a Research Assistant in the Department of Political Science at the University of Geneva. He is preparing a doctoral dissertation on the comparative history of the Labour Movement in the Swiss cantons. He has recently published (with Dominique Wisler) 'Die "Massaker" von 1932. Protest, Diskurs und Oeffentlichkeit', *Swiss Political Science Review*, 4 (1998).

David Waddington is Reader in Communications at Sheffield Hallam University. He has published widely on public order problems, notably *Contemporary Issues in Public Disorder: A Comparative and Historical Approach* (London, 1992) and, with Chas Critcher, *Flashpoints: Studies in Public Disorder* (London, 1989).

Dominique Wisler is a Lecturer in the Department of Political Science at the University of Geneva. He is currently directing a project for the Swiss National Foundation of Science on urban protest and violence. His recent publications include (with Hanspeter Kriesi) 'Direct Democracy and Social Movements in Switzerland', *European Journal of Political Research* 30 (1996), and (with Jose Barranco) 'Validity and Systematicity of Newspaper Data in Event Analysis', *European Sociological Review*, 15, 3 (1999).

Index